An Illustrated Data Guide To

World War II
Maritime
Attack
Aircraft

Compiled by
Christopher Chant

**TIGER BOOKS INTERNATIONAL
LONDON**

This edition published in 1997 by
Tiger Books International PLC
Twickenham

Published in Canada in 1997 by
Vanwell Publishing Limited
St. Catharines, Ontario

© Graham Beehag Books
Christchurch
Dorset

Printed and bound in Hong Kong

ISBN 1-85501-860-8

CONTENTS

Aichi D3A 'Val'

Manufacturer: Aichi Tokei Denki K.K.
(later Aichi Kokuki K.K.)

Country of origin: Japan

Specification: D3A2 Model 22

Type: Carrierborne and land-based dive-bomber

Accommodation: Pilot and radio operator/gunner in tandem in an enclosed cockpit

Entered service: 1940

Left service: August 1945

Armament (fixed): Two 0.303in (7.7mm) Type 97 fixed forward-firing machine-guns with 791 rounds per gun in the upper part of the forward fuselage with synchronisation equipment to fire through the propeller disc, and one 0.303in (7.7mm) Type 92 trainable rearward-firing machine-gun with 582 rounds in the rear cockpit

Armament (disposable): Up to 816lb (370kg) of disposable stores carried on three hardpoints (one under the fuselage rated at 551lb/250kg and two under the wings with each unit rated at 132lb/60kg), and generally comprising one 551lb (250kg) bomb and two 132lb (60kg) bombs

Operational equipment: Standard communication and navigation equipment, plus optical sights

Powerplant: One Mitsubishi Kinsei 54 radial piston engine rated at 1,300hp (969kW) for take-off and 1,200hp (895kW) at 9,845ft (3,000m)

Fuel capacity: Internal fuel 237.35 Imp gal (1,079 litres); external fuel none

Dimensions: Span 47ft 2in (14.365m); aspect ratio 5.91; area 375.66sq ft (34.90sq m); length 33ft 5.375in (10.195m); height 12ft 7.5in (3.847m)

Weights: Empty 5,666lb (2,570kg) equipped; normal take-off 8,378lb (3,800kg); maximum take-off 9,100lb (4,128kg)

Performance: Maximum level speed 'clean' 232kt (267mph; 430km/h) at 20,340ft (6,200m); cruising speed 160kt (184mph; 296km/h) at 9,845ft (3,000m); typical range 730nm (840 miles; 1,352km); climb to 9,845ft (3,000m) in 5min 48sec; service ceiling 34,450ft (10,500m)

Variants

D3A1: In 1936 the Imperial Japanese navy air force decided to update its carrierborne air assets, which were largely of the biplane type with fixed landing gear. The service opined that the imminent availability of aircraft carriers with larger flightdecks combined with the increasing threat posed by land-based monoplane fighters necessitated a rapid move to the monoplane layout. Thus, during the summer of 1936, the navy issued a requirement for a carrierborne monoplane dive-bomber to supersede the Aichi D1A2 biplane dive-bomber that was currently the navy air force's carrierborne mainstay. The three companies that responded to the requirement were Aichi, Mitsubishi and Nakajima, and the first two each received a contract for two prototypes.

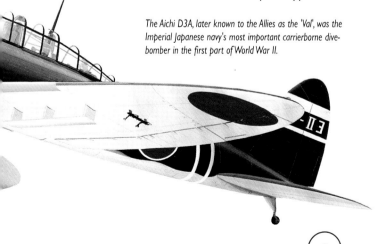

The Aichi D3A, later known to the Allies as the 'Val', was the Imperial Japanese navy's most important carrierborne dive-bomber in the first part of World War II.

Simple and sturdy, the Aichi D3A was a moderately advanced type at the time of its introduction, but was soon rendered obsolete by features such as its fixed main landing gear units, lack of armour protection for the crew and vital systems, and lack of self-sealing fuel tanks.

Aichi's AM-17 design was prepared under the supervision of Tokuhishiro Goake, and the influence exerted by the company's technical association with Heinkel was reflected in the adoption of a monoplane layout with a low-set cantilever wing of elliptical planform – clearly inspired by that of the Heinkel He 70 Blitz. The design team considered retractable landing gear, but decided that the performance advantages accruing from such gear would be more than offset by its weight and more difficult maintenance. The design therefore matured as a basically all-metal type with an oval-section fuselage of the semi-monocoque type, a cantilever tail unit with a mid-set tailplane, a low-set wing, and fixed tailwheel landing gear including wide-track cantilever main units with spatted wheels. The wing was based on a flat centre section of the constant-chord type, and to this were attached the dihedraled elliptical-planform outer

As a mainstay of the Imperial Japanese navy's airstrength, the Aichi D3A (seen here in the form of a D3A1) was flown by well-trained crews who could achieve great bombing accuracy at the end of dives as steep as 80°.

panels, just outboard of the main landing gear units. There were dive brakes under the wings ahead of the outer parts of the flaps, and virtually the full span of the trailing edges was occupied by inboard flaps and outboard ailerons, the latter fabric-covered as were the rudder and elevators.

The first prototype made its maiden flight in January 1938 with a powerplant of one Nakajima Hikari 1 radial piston engine rated at 710hp (529kW) and driving a three-blade metal propeller of the variable-pitch type. The initial trials were disappointing, for the prototype was under-powered, lacked directional stability in turns, and suffered severe vibration problems when the dive brakes were deployed.

Conversely, the prototype revealed great strength and generally good handling characteristics, so Aichi persevered and completed the second prototype to an improved standard, with the Mitsubishi Kinsei 3 radial piston engine rated at 840hp (626kW), a greater vertical tail surface, stronger dive brakes, a wing increased in span from 46ft 3.125in (14.10m) to 47ft 6.875in (14.50m) for an additional 21.528sq ft (2.0sq m) of area, and outboard leading edges that had marked downward camber to reduce the type's tendency to snap-roll in tight turns.

In this form the D3A1 was judged superior to the Nakajima D3N1 and was ordered into production for service with the full designation Navy Type 99 Carrier Bomber Model 11. The production standard differed slightly from that of the second prototype in external details such as a marginally smaller wing, a powerplant of one Kinsei 43

or Kinsei 44 engine rated at 1,000 and 1,070hp (746 and 798kW) respectively, and the introduction of a dorsal fin for final elimination of the directional instability problem. The gun armament was not notably heavy, comprising only three 0.303in (7.7mm) machine-guns arranged as two fixed and one trainable weapon, and the weapons load comprised one 551lb (250kg) bomb carried on a centreline crutch that swung it clear of the propeller disc before release, and two 132lb (60kg) bombs carried under the outer wing panels.

The D3A1 otherwise differed from the later D3A2 in details such as its empty weight of 5,309lb (2,408kg); maximum take-off weight of 8,047lb (3,650kg); maximum level speed of 209kt (240mph; 386km/h) at 9,845ft (3,000m); cruising speed of 160kt (184mph; 296km/h) at 9,845ft (3,000m); range of 795nm (915 miles; 1,472km); climb to 9,845ft (3,000m) in 6min 27sec, and service ceiling of 30,050ft (9,160m).

The D3A1 completed its carrier qualification trials in 1940 and entered service later in the same year, initially seeing service from land bases in the 2nd Sino-Japanese War (1937-45). The D3A1 was in full service when Japan attacked Pearl Harbor in December 1941, and 126 of the type took part in the attack and proved themselves to be excellent dive-bombers. Further evidence of the D3A1's dive-bombing capabilities was provided in the subsequent Japanese carrier foray into the Indian Ocean, when D3A1 warplanes achieved an 87 per cent hit rate on two manoeuvring British cruisers and an 82 per cent hit rate on a British aircraft carrier undertaking evasive manoeuvres.

The D3A1 received the Allied reporting name ëVal', but began to suffer heavy losses in the fighting around Guadalcanal in the Solomon Islands from August 1942. Many experienced aircrews and their aircraft were lost, and the Japanese carrier arm was already in decline after its losses in the Battles of the Coral Sea and Midway in mid-1942. The aircraft were comparatively easy to replace but were now obsolescent, but the new aircrews lacked the skills of their predecessors, and the aircraft carriers could not readily be replaced. Increasingly, therefore, the D3A1 was operated from land bases. Production of the D3A1 between December 1939 and August 1942 totalled 470 aircraft excluding two prototypes and six service trials aircraft.

D3A2: First flown in June 1942 was the sole D3A2 Model 12 prototype that differed from its predecessor in being

Seen here in the form of a restored aeroplane with an American radial engine, the D3A2 was the definitive version of the Aichi D3A carrierborne dive-bomber with features such as a propeller spinner, greater internal fuel capacity, and an improved cockpit canopy. A useful feature from the type's beginning was the use of trailing-edge flaps for improved take-off and landing performance.

powered by the Kinsei 54 radial engine rated at 1,300hp (969kW) and supplied with fuel from an enlarged internal capacity, in having a propeller spinner, and in having a revised canopy with a more acutely angled rear section. This model was ordered into production for service with the full designation Navy Type 99 Carrier Bomber Model 22, and began to reach the squadrons in the autumn of 1942.

Production of this model totalled 1,016 aircraft (815 from Aichi between August 1942 and June 1944, and the other 201 from Showa between December 1942 and August 1945), and the type was the navy's primary dive-bomber until the advent of the superior Yokosuka D4Y Suisei. From this time the D3A2 was increasingly operated from land bases but also from the smaller carriers whose flightdecks were inadequate for the D4Y. A number of the aircraft were converted as trainers under the revised short and full designations D3A2-K and Navy Type 99 Bomber Trainer Model 12 respectively, but during the last 12 months of the war many aircraft were expended in *kamikaze* missions, in which they suffered horrendous losses without tangible result.

Blackburn B-24 Skua

Manufacturer: Blackburn Aircraft Ltd.

Country of origin: UK

Specification: Skua Mk II

Type: Carrierborne and land-based dive-bomber and fighter

Accommodation: Pilot and observer/gunner in an enclosed cockpit

Entered service: November 1938

Left service: 1945

Armament (fixed): Four 0.303in (7.7mm) Browning Mk II fixed forward-firing machine-guns in the wing leading edges, and one 0.303in (7.7mm) Mk IIIE or Vickers 'K' trainable rearward-firing machine-gun on a Fairey pillar-type mounting in the rear cockpit

Armament (disposable): Up to 500lb (227kg) of disposable stores carried on one hardpoint under the fuselage rated at 500lb (227kg), and generally comprising one 500lb (227kg) bomb on a crutch to swing it clear of the propeller disc

Operational equipment: Standard communication and navigation equipment, plus a pilot's reflector sight and gunner's optical sight

Powerplant: One Bristol Perseus XII radial piston engine rated at 890hp (664kW) at 7,000ft (2,134m)

Fuel capacity: Internal fuel not specified; external fuel none

Seen with its flaps lowered to serve as dive brakes, this Blackburn Skua dive-bomber of the Fleet Air Arm reveals first-generation 'modern' monoplane design in the general angularity of its lines, most especially noticeable in a cockpit enclosure that had the look of an additional rather than integral part of the aeroplane.

Dimensions: Span 46ft 2in (14.07m) and width folded 15ft 6in (4.72m); aspect ratio 6.83; area 312.00sq ft (28.98sq m); length 35ft 7in (10.85m); height 12ft 6in (3.81m)

Weights: Empty 5,490lb (2,490kg) equipped; maximum take-off 8,228lb (3,732kg)

Performance: Maximum level speed 'clean' 195kt (225mph; 362km/h) at 6,500ft (1,981m) declining to 177kt (204mph; 328km/h) at sea level; cruising speed, maximum 162kt (187mph; 301km/h) at optimum altitude and economical 99kt (114mph; 183km/h) at optimum altitude; typical range 378nm (435 miles; 700km); maximum rate of climb at sea level 1,580ft (482m) per minute; service ceiling 20,200ft (6,157m)

Variant
Skua Mk II: The Skua has the twin distinctions of having been both the first purpose-designed British dive-bomber

and the first monoplane to enter full service with the Fleet Air Arm. It was also the first aeroplane to enter British carrierborne service with a metal-skinned airframe, retractable landing gear, flaps and a variable-pitch propeller.

The type was designed under the supervision of G.E. Petty to meet the Air Ministry's O.27/34 requirement, and in April 1935 the Ministry ordered two Skua Mk I prototypes after rejecting conceptually similar designs from Avro, Boulton Paul, Hawker and Vickers.

The first of these prototypes made its maiden flight in February 1937 with a powerplant of one Bristol Mercury IX radial piston engine rated at 840hp (626kW) and driving a three-blade de Havilland propeller of the two-pitch type, thus revealing its combination of modern features with some well-proved features. The latter included a semi-monocoque fuselage of the type pioneered in the B-6 Shark, typified by flush-riveted Alclad skinning, two watertight compartments as a buoyancy aid, and a cockpit section that was watertight up to the canopy sills.

The fuselage was of basically circular section and comprised the structural heart of the airframe, which was designed for modern carrierborne operations and was therefore stressed for catapult launches as well as arrested landings. The angular and heavily framed cockpit enclosure gave the impression that it was something of an afterthought as it projected from the upper line of the fuselage in a fashion that induced much drag. The rest of the airframe comprised the tailwheel landing gear with main units that retracted outwards into wells in the undersurfaces of the wings, and the flying surfaces that comprised a cantilever low-set wing and a cantilever tail unit. The wing was of the same type of Alclad-skinned construction as the fuselage, and was built in three sections: the narrow-span, flat centre section was bolted into the lower part of the fuselage below the cockpit section, and supported the tapered and dihedraled outer panels that contained watertight compartments and carried, on their trailing edges, outboard fabric-covered ailerons and inboard Zap flaps that doubled as dive brakes. The outer wing panels folded to the rear, rotating in the process so that their undersurfaces faced outwards, and in the stowed position rested close to the vertical surface of the tail unit, which was located forward of the horizontal surface: these surfaces were of light-alloy construction, and while the fixed surfaces were skinned in Alclad, the control surfaces were covered with fabric.

The type was designed to double as a fighter as well as a dive-bomber, and therefore carried a fixed forward-firing armament of four machine-guns in the wing leading edges to supplement the primary offensive armament of one 500lb (227kg) semi-armour-piercing bomb carried under the fuselage on a crutch that swung it clear of the propeller disc before release. The second prototype joined the trials programme after making its first flight in May 1938, and this machine had its nose lengthened by 2ft 4.75in (0.73m) in the fashion adopted for all later Skuas. Trials revealed the need for few changes, although the Skua Mk I's mild stalling characteristics meant that the leading-edge slots could be removed, and production of the Skua Mk II proceeded without delay to meet an order that had been placed in July 1936 for 190 aircraft.

The Skua Mk II's primary differences from the Skua Mk I second prototype were upturned wingtips, a changed oleo in the tailwheel to eliminate juddering, and a different powerplant in the form of the Bristol Perseus XII radial piston engine rated at 890hp (664kW) (the Mercury having been scheduled for use in the Bristol Type 142 Blenheim light bomber series). The first Skua Mk II flew in August 1938, and all 190 aircraft were delivered between October 1938 and March 1940. The two Fleet Air Arm units to receive the new warplane were Nos 800 and 803 Squadrons on the carrier HMS *Courageous*, on which the Skua Mk II replaced the Hawker Nimrod and Hawker Osprey.

By the time of the outbreak of World War II (1939-45), the Skua Mk II was also operational with No. 801 Squadron on the carrier HMS *Furious* and with the shore-based No. 806 Squadron. By the beginning of the war the obsolescence of the Skua Mk II as a fighter had already been recognised, so the type was used exclusively as a dive-bomber.

The Skua Mk II's greatest success was the sinking of the cruiser KMS *Königsberg* during the German invasion of Norway that began in April 1940, but the type's limitations were cruelly revealed only a few days later when many aircraft were lost in an attack on the German forces in Narvik. The Skua Mk II was withdrawn from first-line service in 1941, when Nos 800 and 806 Squadrons re-equipped with the Fairey Fulmar, and Nos 801 and 803 Squadrons switched to the Hawker Sea Hurricane. The aircraft served thereafter as target tug and utility aircraft.

Bristol Type 152 Beaufort

Manufacturer: Bristol Aeroplane Co. Ltd.

Country of origin: UK

Specification: Beaufort Mk I

Type: Torpedo bomber

Accommodation: Pilot and navigator/bombardier side by side in an enclosed cockpit, radar/radio operator in the fuselage, and gunner in the dorsal turret

Entered service: January 1940

Left service: 1947

Armament (fixed): Two 0.303in (7.7mm) Vickers 'K' trainable forward-firing machine-guns in the nose with 300 rounds per gun, or in later aircraft two 0.303in (7.7mm) Browning fixed forward-firing machine-guns in the wing leading edges with 300 rounds (port) and 500 rounds (starboard); two 0.303in (7.7mm) Vickers 'K' trainable rearward-firing machine-guns with 900 rounds per gun in the power-operated Bristol B.IV Mk I or Mk IE dorsal turret, or in later aircraft two 0.303in (7.7mm) Browning trainable rearward-firing machine-guns with 950 rounds per gun in the power-operated Bristol B.I Mk V dorsal turret; two 0.303in (7.7mm) Vickers 'K' trainable lateral-firing machine-guns with 250 rounds per gun in two beam positions and, in some later aircraft, one 0.303in (7.7mm) Browning trainable rearward-firing machine-gun with 600 rounds in the undernose blister position

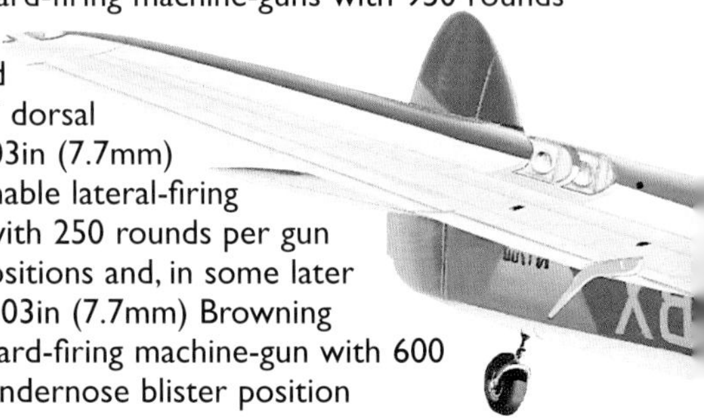

Armament (disposable): Up to 2,000lb (907kg) of disposable stores carried in a lower-fuselage weapons bay rated at 2,000lb (907kg), and generally comprising one 1,605lb (728kg) 18in (457mm) Mk XII torpedo, or one 1,500lb (680kg) Mk I mine, or one 2,000lb (907kg) bomb, or two 1,000lb (454kg) bombs, or four 500lb (227kg) bombs, or eight 250lb (113kg) bombs

Operational equipment: Standard communication and navigation equipment, plus an optical bomb sight, optical gunsights, ASV.Mk II air-to-surface search radar, F.24 reconnaissance camera for oblique or ventral photography, and F.46 camera for strike photography

Powerplant: Two Bristol Taurus II or VI radial piston engines each rated at 860hp (641kW) for take-off and 1,065hp (794kW) for emergencies, or alternatively two Bristol Taurus XII or XVI radial piston engines each rated at 1,085hp (809kW) for take-off and 1,130hp (843kW) for emergencies

Fuel capacity: Internal fuel 570 Imp gal (2,591.2 litres) plus provision for up to 138 Imp gal (627.3 litres) of auxiliary fuel in one optional weapons-bay tank; external fuel none

Dimensions: Span 57ft 10in (17.63m); aspect ratio 7.42; area 451.00sq ft (41.89sq m); length 44ft 2in (13.46m); height 15ft 10in (4.83m); wheel track 18ft 0in (5.49m)

Weights: Empty 11,739lb (5,325kg) equipped; normal take-off 14,074lb (6,384kg) as a torpedo bomber; maximum take-off 17,700lb (8,029kg)

Performance: Maximum level speed 'clean' 234kt (270mph; 434km/h) at 10,000ft (3,048m) declining to 225kt (259mph; 417km/h) at 2,000ft (610m); cruising speed, maximum 223kt (257mph; 414km/h) at 10,000ft (3,048m) and economical 174kt (200mph; 322km/h) at optimum altitude; maximum range 1,389.5nm (1,600 miles; 2,575km); typical range 899nm (1,035 miles; 1,666km); endurance 6hr 0min; maximum rate of climb at sea level 1,450ft (442m) per minute; climb to 15,000ft (4,572m) in 13min 30sec; service ceiling 19,700ft (6,005m)

Variants
Beaufort Mk I: In the mid-1930s the aerial protection of the British coast against naval attack was entrusted to a small number of obsolescent or obsolete biplanes, although the new Avro Type 652 Anson was on the verge of entering service as the RAF's first monoplane general reconnaissance (or coastal patrol) type. Despite the fact that it was only approaching its service debut, the Anson was regarded as merely an interim type, and in the summer of 1935 the Air Ministry issued two requirements for advanced warplanes: the M.15/35 requirement called for a three-seat torpedo bomber to replace the Vickers Type 206 Vildebeest, and the G.24/35 requirement demanded a four-seat general reconnaissance type to succeed the Anson.

Despite the fact that the British aero industry numbered some 20 aircraft manufacturers at this time, the only three who evinced any real interest in the two requirements were Avro, Blackburn and Bristol. Avro was concerned to maintain the position it had secured with the Anson and tendered its Type 672 as a derivative of the Anson with an uprated powerplant of two Armstrong Siddeley Terrier radial piston engines; Blackburn wished to secure the same type of land-based niche as it already possessed with its carrierborne and shore-based torpedo bombers, and therefore projected a high-wing monoplane with internal torpedo accommodation.

Bristol, on the other hand, was new to the whole field of maritime aircraft and was interested in gaining a foothold in both markets, and considered its ideal starting point to be the Type 142M low-wing monoplane under development for service with the RAF as the Blenheim Mk I light bomber. Towards the end of 1935, therefore, Bristol approached the Air Ministry with two related designs evolved ultimately from the Type 142M. The Type 149 was suggested as the

Seen in the markings of No. 217 Squadron, one of six RAF Coastal Command units to operate the type in northern Europe, this is a Bristol Beaufort Mk I torpedo bomber. Note the twin-gun dorsal turret at the rear of the raised superstructure section.

answer to the G.24/35 requirement on the basis of a Blenheim Mk I with a wider fuselage, a four-man crew (pilot, navigator/bombardier, radio operator and gunner), three 0.303in (7.7mm) machine-guns in the form of one fixed forward-firing weapon in the port wing and two trainable weapons in a power-operated dorsal turret, the same weapons bay as the Blenheim Mk I, and a powerplant of two Bristol Aquila AE3M radial piston engines for an estimated maximum level speed of 220.5kt (254mph; 409km/h) at optimum altitude after take-off at a maximum weight of 10,930lb (4,958kg).

The Type 150 was put forward as the solution to the M.15/35 requirement on the basis of a slightly enlarged Blenheim Mk I airframe, with span increased to 58ft 0in (17.68m) and length increased to 44ft 3in (13.49m), a crew of three (pilot who aimed and launched the torpedo, radio operator who had to move forward from the central fuselage into the nose to act as the bombardier when required, and dorsal gunner), and a powerplant of two Bristol Perseus VI radial piston engines each rated at 890hp (664kW) for an estimated maximum level speed of 243kt (280mph; 450km/h) at 5,000ft (1,524m) with a 1,900lb (862kg) torpedo.

With these two proposals in the hands of the Air Ministry, the design team headed by Leslie Frise suggested early in 1936 that the core similarity between the Type 149 and Type 150 would make it possible to produce a single design that, with minimum modifications, could satisfy both requirements: the main change foreseen was the raising of the cabin floor in the torpedo bomber version to provide additional depth in the weapons bay below it, even though the torpedo would still have to be carried in a semi-exposed position.

This revised Type 152 proposal was submitted to the Air Ministry in April 1936, and other changes incorporated at this time were a lengthened nose to provide an effective navigator/bombardier position, and the relocation of the radio/camera position to a point just forward of the dorsal turret so that the gunner could double as the radio/camera operator and thus obviate the need for a fourth crew member. The Type 152 was offered with alternative powerplants in the form of two Aquila AE3M or Perseus VI radial engines for maximum take-off weights of 10,990lb (4,985kg) or 12,240lb (5,552kg) respectively, the latter offering significantly higher performance despite its greater weight.

For obvious financial and operational reasons, the Air Ministry fully approved of the concept of a single warplane able to undertake the general reconnaissance and torpedo bomber roles, and the Type 152 proposal was used in the finalisation of Specification 10/36, which called for a number of changes of which the most important was a four-man crew: the Bristol team provided the required accommodation by increasing the height of the central fuselage, which was now faired into the forward edge of the

dorsal turret with useful benefits in drag reduction. This meant that the cockpit was above the forward end of the weapons bay with the radio operator's position behind it. Avro and Blackburn were still interested in the requirement, the former revising its Type 672 to Type 675 standard and the latter upgrading its original design to B-26 standard.

At a time of increasing European crisis, so pressing were the demands of the RAF's coastal squadrons for advanced new aircraft that the Type 152 and B-26 were ordered into production 'off the drawing board' as the Beaufort and Botha respectively, each with a powerplant of two Perseus radial engines. In 1937, however, reassessment of the Beaufort and the Botha suggested that their performance figures would fall below those of the Blenheim light bomber, which was already giving some cause for concern.

The obvious alternative was the new Bristol Taurus radial piston engine rated at 1,150hp (857kW), but this engine had not yet been type-tested, so the Air Ministry therefore decided that the Botha would have to retain the Perseus powerplant (which effectively killed the type as a useful operational warplane) while the Beaufort switched to the Taurus powerplant. In general terms, the Beaufort retained a close design and structural relationship with the Blenheim, although it had the larger wing and longer fuselage originally proposed for the Type 150.

The Beaufort was of all-metal construction using the stressed-skin structural concept, and was a cantilever mid/low-wing monoplane with metal-framed but fabric-covered control surfaces, split flaps along the full span of the wing trailing edges inboard of the ailerons, and tailwheel landing gear whose main units retracted rearward into the after portion of

This is a Bristol Beaufort Mk I of No. 42 Squadron, RAF Coastal Command. The type's close relationship to another pair of Bristol warplanes, the Blenheim light bomber and the Beaufighter heavy fighter, is clearly evident in the shaping of the nose, outer wing panels and tail unit as well as in the general configuration of the aeroplane.

The Bristol Beaufort Mk I torpedo bomber of the RAF was powered by two Bristol Taurus XII radial piston engines, and had only marginally adequate power for an aeroplane of its size and weight, meaning that performance and agility were affected. These are Beauforts being readied for a training mission by naval personnel, who are loading a dummy torpedo.

the two engine nacelles underslung from the wing leading edges. The weapons bay was large enough to accommodate a single 2,000lb (907kg) bomb once this had become available, but the originally planned alternative to one torpedo or a single mine was just two 500lb (227kg) or four 250lb (113kg) bombs. Similarly, the originally schemed defensive armament comprised one 0.303in (7.7mm) Browning fixed forward-firing machine-gun in the port wing and two 0.303in (7.7mm) Browning trainable rearward-firing machine-guns in the Bristol B.IV Mk I dorsal turret: there were inadequate supplies of the Browning, so early aircraft carried one or two 0.303in (7.7mm) Vickers 'K' machine-guns in the turret, and the gun armament was later comprehensively strengthened.

Several refinements were made to facilitate construction: the most notable of these was final assembly from a number of comparatively small subassemblies, and this was intended to allow the major part of construction to be undertaken by subcontractors. The decision to omit the prototype stage had been taken in the interests of speeding the production programme and thus securing an early service debut, so an intensive development programme was planned for the first five aircraft to emerge from the initial Beaufort production order: this amounted to 78 aircraft ordered in August 1936 with a powerplant of two Taurus II moderately supercharged or Taurus III fully supercharged radial engines each driving a three-blade de Havilland propeller of the constant-speed type. The whole engine installation, complete with its cowling, was designed by the Bristol engine division, and needed considerable development to prevent engine overheating; this fact, combined with the need to disperse Blenheim production

to government-funded 'shadow factories' so that Bristol could maintain adequate production-line space, delayed the appearance of the first Beaufort Mk I until August 1938.

Finalisation of the solution to the cooling gill problem occupied a further two months, so the Beaufort Mk I made its first flight in October 1938. Flight trials then revealed other problems, requiring the replacement of the single apron-like door attached to the front of each main landing gear unit by a pair of conventional doors on the sides of each gear-well, and the relocation of the engine exhausts.

It was January 1940 before the Beaufort Mk I finally entered service with No. 22 Squadron of RAF Coastal Command. The squadron flew its first operational sortie with the Beaufort Mk I in April 1940, laying mines in German coastal waters, but in the following months all the aircraft were grounded as a result of engine problems. At this time the first aircraft had been completed either with the Taurus III radial engine and the designation Beaufort Mk I, or with the Taurus II radial engine and the designation Beaufort Mk II. It was evident, however, that the Beaufort's generally low-level role did not require the use of fully supercharged engines, so the Taurus II was standardised, and the Taurus III engines of completed aircraft were adapted to Taurus II standard with cropped supercharger impeller blades and the designation Taurus IIA: the planned Beaufort Mk II designation was then discontinued (but was used by a later development).

From the middle of 1940 all new aircraft were delivered with the Taurus VI, a version of the Taurus II with features optimising it for use in the Beaufort Mk I, and later aircraft were delivered with the Taurus XII or Taurus XVI, which were versions of the Taurus II and Taurus VI respectively with an improved crankshaft. By the time that the Beaufort Mk I was entering service, orders for the type had been increased to 350 from Bristol and a further 90 (with an option for another 10) had been ordered from the Australian production line (as detailed below) for delivery in the Far East to boost the British military capability in Malaya. In the event, only six of these Australian-built aircraft had reached Malaya, where the type was due to re-equip Nos 36 and 100 Squadrons, before the Japanese attack on Pearl Harbor in December 1941. Five of the aircraft were then returned to Australia, and all further Australian production was reserved for the Royal Australian Air Force.

To replace the 90 Australian-built aircraft, the Air Ministry ordered 90 more Beaufort Mk Is from Bristol, which completed 85 to this standard and the last five as Beaufort Mk IIs. Further contracts were placed, bringing production of the Beaufort Mk I to an eventual figure of 1,014. As a result of the design of the aeroplane for final assembly from subcontracted assemblies, production of the

This is an example of the Bristol Beaufort Mk II with a powerplant of two Pratt & Whitney R-1830 Twin Wasp radial piston engines driving Curtiss Electric three-blade propellers of the constant-speed type. The location is one of the blast-proof pens at Luqa in Malta, from which units such as No. 86 Squadron wrought havoc on Axis convoys crossing the Mediterranean.

Beaufort Mk I peaked at 30 aircraft per month only five months after the delivery of the first machine, and this was a record for British aircraft production in World War II.

As these aircraft were being produced, operational experience and continued development combined to yield a number of improved features. The first major alteration was a change from the original type of curved bomb-aiming window to a flat panel offering better optical charac-teristics, and this was followed by the addition of a second fixed forward-firing machine-gun (in the starboard wing to match the original weapon in the port wing) with provision for these two weapons to be replaced by two Vickers 'K' machine-guns on gimbal mountings in the navigator/-bombardier's position in the nose; other features included the incorporation of a blister fairing under the nose with a single Browning trainable rearward-firing machine-gun for ventral defence that was then supp-lemented and often replaced by two Vickers 'K' trainable lateral-firing machine-guns operated by the radio operator from two beam positions in his compartment; the replacement of the original dorsal turret by a Bristol B.I Mk V turret with two Browning machine-guns; the installation of ASV.Mk II air-to-surface search radar with Yagi antennae under the wings and nose; the adoption of small trailing-edge plates of almost semi-circular shape behind the engine nacelles to smooth the airflow over the tailplane and thus reduce buffet; the sealing of the unsuccessful Youngman pneumatically operated dive brakes on the wing trailing edges and their omission from later production aircraft; and the adoption of a retractable tailwheel in place of the original fixed unit.

Production of the Beaufort series in the UK ended with the last Beaufort Mk I, which was delivered at the end of 1943. The Beaufort Mk I was operated by three air forces in addition to the RAF. Some 18 aircraft were transferred late in 1941 to the South African Air Force, which allocated the type to No. 36 and part of No. 37 Coastal Defence Flights, which were later merged to become No. 20 Squadron that was itself renamed No. 16 Squadron in September 1942, just two months before the SAAF phased the Beaufort Mk I out of service. Another 15 aircraft were supplied to the Royal Canadian Air Force in August 1941 and equipped No. 149 (Torpedo Bomber) Squadron until October 1944. Finally, 12 Beaufort Mk Is were delivered to Turkey late in 1944, but saw only limited use.

In it basic configuration the Bristol Beaufort, seen here in the form of a Beaufort Mk I of No.217 Squadron, bore a very strong similarity to the Beaufighter heavy fighter except for its central fuselage's raised upper line ending in the power-operated dorsal turret.

Beaufort Mk II: All the improved features added sequentially in the Beaufort Mk I were retrofitted on or built into the Beaufort Mk II, which was a development of the Beaufort Mk I with a different powerplant (as there were fears that production of the Taurus radial engine might lag behind that of the Beaufort airframe). The engine selected for the revised powerplant was an American radial piston engine, the Pratt & Whitney R-1830-S3C4G Twin Wasp rated at 1,200hp (895kW) for take-off and driving a three-blade Curtiss Electric metal propeller of the constant-speed type. The inspiration for this selection was the Australian Beaufort Mk V, for which the Twin Wasp had earlier been chosen because deliveries of the Taurus to Australia were slow and difficult: the Australians decided to adopt the Twin Wasp in a licence-made form as this offered greater power and could be used in a number of other warplanes.

The first Beaufort Mk II was a converted Beaufort Mk I with imported American engines, and this made its maiden flight in November 1940. The first production-line machine flew in September 1941 and revealed improved performance, especially at take-off. Production totalled only 165 aircraft, however, as supplies of the Taurus matched those of the airframe and the improved Taurus XII and Taurus XVI radial engines were available for installation in place of the imported engines.

The Beaufort Mk II was dimensionally identical with the Beaufort Mk I, but differed in details such as its empty weight of 12,742lb (5,780kg); maximum take-off weight of 21,000lb (9,526kg); maximum level speed of 226kt (260mph; 418km/h) at 14,500ft (4,420m) with a torpedo; maximum cruising speed of 200kt (230mph; 370km/h) at 6,500ft (1,981m) with a torpedo; typical range of 1,259nm (1,450 miles; 2,333km), and service ceiling of 18,000ft (5,486m). Although only 164 Beaufort Mk IIs came off the production line at Filton, another 250 aircraft were assembled in 1943 and 1944 at Bristol's Banwell facility, and the last of these machines was completed in November 1944 to end British production of the Beaufort after the delivery of 1,429 aircraft.

Most of the aircraft delivered from Banwell were not operational machines – the Beaufort having been replaced by the Bristol Beaufighter in Coastal Command squadrons by this time – but were Beaufort Mk II(T) trainers delivered to operational conversion units. These aircraft were fitted with dual flying controls, and lacked the dorsal turret and other operational equipment of the basic Beaufort Mk II. Some 12 of these aircraft were supplied to the Turkish air force in 1945, and remained in service up to 1947. In overall terms, the Beaufort served with six squadrons of RAF Coastal Command for operations in northern European waters, and also with four squadrons for operations in the Mediterranean theatre, where Malta-based Beauforts were the scourge of the Axis convoys that ferried supplies and equipment to the German and Italian forces in North Africa.

As noted above, from 1943 the Beaufort was replaced in operational units by the more versatile Beaufighter, and the last aircraft were retired in 1944. British models that did not enter production were the Beaufort Mk III with a powerplant of two Rolls-Royce Merlin XXX inverted-Vee piston engines and additional fuel tankage in the outer wing panels for increased range, and the Beaufort Mk IV with a new dorsal turret in the form of the Bristol B.XV carrying four 0.303in (7.7mm) Browning machine-guns and the revised powerplant of two Taurus XX radial engines each rated at 1,250hp (932kW) and driving a three-blade propeller of the constant-speed type. Some 400 examples of the Beaufort Mk IV were ordered in

1942, but the only example to be flown was a Beaufort Mk II prototype conversion.

DAP Beaufort: In 1939 a British air mission travelled to Australia with the twin objectives of assessing how Britain and Australia could make a joint contribution towards regional defence, and how the small Australian aero industry could be developed to supplement the output of the British and other dominion aero industries. The background to this mission's task was provided by the threat to European stability posed by German territorial ambitions, and by the growing threat to Asian stability caused by Japanese territorial and economic ambitions, already evidenced by its occupation of Manchuria, invasion of China and desire for the raw materials to be found in South-East Asia and the myriad islands of the Netherlands East Indies.

The Beaufort seemed an ideal selection for Australian manufacture: its design for subcontracted manufacture accorded well with the fragmented and currently limited nature of the Australian aero industry, and its production would allow the RAF to bolster its defences in South-East Asia and help the expanding RAAF to develop a potent anti-ship capability that could be decisive against any Japanese campaign dependent on amphibious operations. Supervision of the production programme was entrusted to the Department of Aircraft Production (DAP), which created a Beaufort Division to oversee the construction of an initial batch of 180 Beaufort Mk I aircraft for final assembly at two facilities (the Commonwealth Aircraft Corporation at Fishermen's Bend near Melbourne in Victoria, and a new DAP centre at Mascot in New South Wales).

Half of this initial batch was intended for the RAF, which needed to replace the wholly obsolete Vickers Vildebeest biplane torpedo bombers currently operated by Nos 36 and 100 Squadrons based at Singapore. While the bulk of production was to be undertaken fully in Australia, key items that were to be supplied from the UK included the engine, turret, instruments and a few significant structural items. As a boost to Australian production, the British supplied one airframe and kits of components for a further 20 aircraft.

After the outbreak of World War II, however, the DAP became concerned that the delivery of Taurus engines could be interrupted by military and industrial pressure on the United Kingdom, and accordingly began to consider an alternative powerplant. By the end of 1939, the decision had

Seen here in pristine factory-delivery condition, this Bristol Beaufort Mk I has a Bristol B.1 Mk V dorsal turret and is equipped with air-to-surface search radar as indicated by the antennae under the forward fuselage and outer wing panels.

been taken in favour of the R-1830-S3C4G version of the Pratt & Whitney Twin Wasp radial engine rated at 1,200hp (895kW) for take-off, but imports of the Taurus continued for the 90 aircraft being built against the British half of the initial order. It was hoped that this arrangement would allow production to continue whilst alterations to the American powerplant were being completed, but the German invasion of western Europe in May 1940 proved so threatening that Britain halted all further exports of war material, and it was decided that Australian production would be of the variant with a powerplant of two Twin Wasp radial engines (to which the Air Ministry had already allocated the designation Beaufort Mk II).

The Air Ministry then increased its order from 90 to 100 Australian-built Beaufort Mk IIs, excluding that part of the order comprising the similar Beaufort Mk V version for the RAAF. The first flight of the pattern airframe delivered from Britain did not take place until May 1941 as a result of delays occasioned by the switch to the American powerplant, and the first Australian-built Beaufort Mk II flew in August 1941. At least 13 of these Beaufort Mk IIs were completed: six were shipped to Singapore, and one was destroyed after a reconnaissance mission over Thailand before the other five were returned to Australia. The 12 or more remaining aircraft were later revised to Beaufort Mk V standard and were flown in Australian markings to supplement the machines built as Beaufort Mk Vs.

About 37 of these aircraft were completed with a powerplant of two R-1830-S3C4G radial engines built in Australia by General Motors-Holden Ltd., and each driving a Curtiss Electric propeller, but a shortage of this engine type led to the completion of the next 100 aircraft with a powerplant of two imported R-1830-S1C3G radial engines: of these 100 aircraft, 40 were completed with Curtiss Electric propellers (with the designation Beaufort Mk VI), and the other 60 were completed with Hamilton Standard propellers (with the designation Beaufort Mk VII). Renewed supplies of Australian-built engines resulted in the Beaufort Mk VA, of which 30 were produced with Hamilton Standard Hydromatic propellers, to complete the original order for 180 aircraft.

Orders were then placed for an additional 520 aircraft that were delivered between November 1942 and August 1944 to the definitive Beaufort Mk VIII standard, with a powerplant of two Australian-built engines each driving a Curtiss Electric propeller; ASV.Mk II radar; provision for both American and British disposable loads (bombs and torpedoes); gimbal-mounted nose guns rather than wing-mounted weapons; additional fuel tankage in the outer wing panels for extended range; and the Bristol B.I Mk V dorsal turret with two 0.303in (7.7mm) Browning machine-guns or, in the last 140 aircraft, the Australian-built Bristol B.I Mk VE dorsal turret with two 0.5in (12.7mm) Browning machine-guns.

In the last months of World War II, some 46 of the Beaufort Mk VIII aircraft were revised to Beaufort Mk IX standard as passenger and/or freight transports with the dorsal turret removed and the upper line of the fuselage faired towards the leading edge of the fin, which was of the Australian type with a forward-bulged leading edge providing the additional area required for effective directional stability in flight with one engine shut down.

The RAAF formed its first Beaufort unit as No. 100 Squadron in March 1942, and this squadron entered service off New Guinea in June 1942. The squadron was the RAAF's sole Beaufort unit until the spring of 1943, when the production rate was sufficient to allow Nos 6 and 8 Squadrons to convert for service later in the year, and to permit the allocation of some aircraft to Nos 7 and 14 Squadrons to supplement their Lockheed Hudsons for reconnaissance work off northern Australia. From late in 1943 the Beauforts of the RAAF were used as much for land bombing as for maritime work, and this tendency increased towards the end of the war, when the Beaufort force had been supplemented by Nos 1, 2, 13, 15 and 32 Squadrons. The last Beauforts were retired from Australian service in 1946.

Bristol Type 156 Beaufighter Mks VI and X

Manufacturer: Bristol Aeroplane Co. Ltd.

Country of origin: UK

Specification: Beaufighter TF.Mk X

Type: Anti-ship attack fighter

Accommodation: Pilot in an enclosed cockpit, and radio operator/radar operator/gunner in the fuselage

Entered service: Early 1942

Left service: Early 1960s

Armament (fixed): Four 20mm Hispano fixed forward-firing cannon with 283 rounds per gun in the underside of the forward fuselage, and one 0.303in (7.7mm) Vickers 'K' trainable rearward-firing machine-gun with 500 rounds in the dorsal position

Armament (disposable): Up to 2,450lb (1,111kg) of disposable stores carried on three hardpoints (one under the fuselage rated at 2,150lb/975kg and two under the wings with each unit rated at 500lb/227kg), and generally comprising one 1,650lb (748kg) or 2,127lb (965kg) torpedo under the fuselage and two 250lb (113kg) bombs or eight 90lb (41kg) rockets under the wings

Operational equipment: Standard communication and navigation equipment, plus a reflector gunsight and AI.Mk VIII search radar

Powerplant: Two Bristol Hercules XVII radial piston engines each rated at 1,770hp (1,320kW) at 7,500ft (2,286m)

Fuel capacity: Internal fuel 624 Imp gal (2,836.7 litres); external fuel up to 200 Imp gal (909.2 litres) in one overload tank carried on the torpedo shackles

One of the finest warplanes of World War II, the Bristol Beaufighter was a powerful and comparatively large two-seat machine used in the night-fighter and maritime attack fighter roles, the latter being illustrated by this Beaufighter TF.Mk 10 with an underfuselage torpedo and provision for rockets under the outer wing panels.

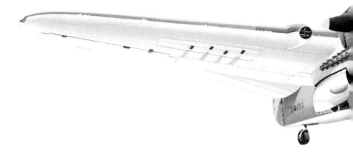

Dimensions: Span 57ft 10in (17.63m); aspect ratio 6.65; area 503.00sq ft (46.73sq m); length 41ft 8in (12.70m); height 15ft 10in (4.83m)

Weights: Empty 15,600lb (7,076kg) equipped; normal take-off 22,600lb (10,251kg); maximum take-off 25,200lb (11,431kg)

Performance: Maximum level speed 'clean' 276kt (318mph; 512km/h) at 10,000ft (3,048m) declining to 263kt (303mph; 488km/h) at 1,300ft (396m); cruising speed, maximum 216kt (249mph; 401km/h) at 4,000ft (1,219m) and economical 178kt (205mph; 330km/h) at 5,000ft (1,524m); maximum range 1,572nm (1,810 miles; 2,913km); typical range 1,277nm (1,470 miles; 2,366km) with a torpedo; climb to 5,000ft (1,524m) in 3min 30sec; service ceiling 15,000ft (4,572m)

Variants

Beaufighter Mk VIC: Although the Type 156 Beaufighter heavy fighter had originally been schemed as a derivative of the Type 152 Beaufort torpedo bomber with a smaller fuselage and an uprated powerplant of two Bristol Hercules VI radial piston engines, this engine type had not been available when the Type 156 was ready for production as the Beaufighter Mk I night-fighter, so the early aircraft were built with a powerplant of two Hercules III radial engines, which were replaced later in the type's production career by a more powerful development of the same basic mark (and

also by a version of the Rolls-Royce Merlin Vee piston engine). By early 1941, however, production of the Hercules series was increasing rapidly to meet requirements for several types, including some important bombers, and the Hercules VI then became available for use in the Beaufighter.

This resulted in the evolution of the Beaufighter Mk VI that was essentially the Beaufighter Mk I with a powerplant of two Hercules VI radial engines each rated at 1,670hp (1,245kW) at 7,500ft (2,286m) and 1,500hp (1,118kW) at 17,000ft (5,181m) or, in some later aircraft, two examples of the Hercules XVI radial engine that was a development of the Hercules VI with a fully automatic mixture carburettor and ratings of 1,675hp (1,249kW) at 6,000ft (1,829m) and 1,410hp (1,051kW) at 14,250ft (4,343m). The new powerplant was evaluated in three Beaufighter Mk I conversions, and demonstrated a modest but nonetheless useful improvement in performance over the basic Beaufighter Mk I.

The Beaufighter Mk VIF accordingly superseded the Beaufighter Mks I and II in production from late in 1941, and the new fighter entered service from early 1942 as a night-fighter with a number of features that had been pioneered on the Mk I series, most notably the dihedraled tailplane to improve stability and control, as well as improved radar in the form of the centimetric-wavelength AI.Mk VII (and later the upgraded AI.Mk VIII) equipments that used an antenna located in a nose-mounted 'thimble' radome to replace the nose- and wing-mounted antennae associated with the AI.Mk IV equipment used in the Beaufighter Mks IF and IIF.

The Beaufighter Mk VIC was the Hercules VI-powered counterpart of the Beaufighter Mk IC, and was thus a longer-range version of the Mk VIF optimised for the attack role in the hands of RAF Coastal Command squadrons. There was provision for the battery of six 0.303in (7.7mm) machine-guns in the wing to be replaced by tankage for an additional 74 Imp gal (336.4 litres) resulting in an increase in range to 1,572nm (1,810 miles; 2,913km) at an economical cruising speed of 211kt (243mph; 391km/h), and in aircraft delivered from May 1943 the outer wing panels were also revised with hardpoints for two 250lb (113kg) bombs or eight 60lb (27kg) rockets, the latter proving quite devastating in the anti-ship role.

Production of the Beaufighter Mk VIC amounted to 693 aircraft delivered by Bristol (518 machines produced in the 'shadow factory' at Weston-super-Mare) and Fairey (175 machines from the 'shadow factory' at Stockport).

Beaufighter Mk VI (ITF): More than a year before the adoption of underwing rocket armament, another addition to the Beaufighter's weapon inventory had made its first appearance. This was the air-launched torpedo, and Bristol began the evolution for such an installation in response to the Air Ministry's suggestion that the Beaufighter could make an effective replacement for the similarly sized Bristol

Seen with the black-and-white 'D-Day markings' introduced in June 1944, this is a Bristol Beaufighter TF.Mk X carrying eight 60lb (27kg) rockets under its outer wing panels.

Beaufort, as it was more economical in crew (two rather than four men), had significantly higher performance as a result of its more potent powerplant, was more agile, and carried notably greater firepower in its gun armament.

Bristol's proposal for the addition of torpedo armament was based on the carriage under the fuselage of the standard British 18in (457mm) torpedo, which weighed 1,650lb (748kg), and would be fitted in this application with an aerodynamic tail unit that would stabilise the weapon in the air but would break off as the torpedo entered the water, and on the adoption of pneumatically operated Youngman air brakes (as designed for the Beaufort but later sealed shut or omitted) on the wing trailing edges to provide the pilot with a steadier run-in to the torpedo release point in either level or diving flight.

The Air Ministry approved the complete installation in April 1943, and one Beaufighter Mk VIC was converted as the prototype in just under two weeks: in its definitive form the underfuselage attachment system could take the 1,650lb (748kg) Mk XII torpedo or a 2,127lb (965kg) American weapon of 22.5in (571mm) calibre.

The prototype conversion was lost during its trials as a result of an engine failure, but had demonstrated its capabilities sufficiently for an order to be placed for an initial 16 Beaufighter Mk VI (ITF) or Interim Torpedo Fighter

aircraft for use by a trials squadron. The aircraft entered service with No. 254 Squadron before the end of 1943, and were followed by another 34 aircraft to the same standard from the Weston-super-Mare factory.

Beaufighter TF.Mk X: Although the Beaufighter Mk VI (ITF) soon proved itself to be all that Coastal Command could have wanted in the way of a replacement for the Beaufort, crews were critical of the retention of the Hercules VI radial engine. This was rated at too high an altitude for most Coastal Command operations, and the result was the evolution of the Hercules VI into the Hercules XVII with cropped supercharger impeller blades and the supercharger locked in medium ratio for the delivery of maximum power at lower altitudes. The adoption of the Hercules XVII in the Beaufighter Mk VI (ITF) airframe resulted in the Beaufighter TF.Mk X torpedo fighter, which was also upgraded with additional cannon ammunition (283 rounds rather than 240 rounds per gun to compensate for the loss of the wing-mounted machine-guns) and a 0.303in (7.7mm) Vickers 'K' trainable rearward-firing machine-gun in the dorsal position as a 'stinger' to deter stern attacks in the upper hemisphere: this dorsal installation was also retrofitted in the Beaufighter Mk VIC and Beaufighter Mk VI (ITF). Two 500lb (227kg) bombs could be carried as an alternative to the torpedo, and the Beaufighter TF.Mk X could also carry two 250lb (113kg) bombs or eight 60lb (27kg) rockets.

Powerful and with a look of total aggression, this is a Bristol Beaufighter TF.Mk X maritime attack fighter of No. 236 Squadron, one of 13 RAF Coastal Command units that operated this potent warplane over northern European waters from bases in the United Kingdom. The type was also operated in the Middle East and Far East with a high level of operational success.

Another fortuitous improvement resulted from the appreciation that the AI.Mk VIII airborne interception radar, as installed in later Mk VIF night-fighters, could also be used in the air-to-surface vessel role: AI.Mk VIII was therefore installed in the Beaufighter TF.Mk X, giving this type a continued ship-detection capability at a time when Germany had evolved countermeasures against earlier types of air-to-surface vessel radar.

Adoption of the torpedo armament had increased the maximum take-off weight of the TF.Mk X to a figure well above that originally envisaged for the Beaufighter series, and an unfortunate consequence was a deterioration of the warplane's handling characteristics: this was the reason for the addition of a long dorsal fin (first evaluated on a Beaufighter Mk IIF) to eliminate the TF.Mk X's tendency to swing on take-off, and elevators of increased area to ensure adequate stability in the pitching plane. As a first step to the introduction of the Beaufighter TF.Mk X, all surviving Mk VI (ITF)s were upgraded with the Hercules XVII powerplant, and then production from the factories at Weston-super-Mare (2,095 machines) and Stoke-on-Trent (110 machines) resulted in a total of 2,205 Beaufighter TF.Mk Xs that were delivered up to September 1945.

This Bristol Beaufighter TF.Mk X carries a potent torpedo under its fuselage, but despite the weight of this weapon, which could weigh up to some 2,200lb (998kg), the aircraft remained fast and relatively manoeuvrable.

These aircraft played a major part in the closing stages of World War II, when the Beaufighter TF.Mk Xs were allocated to special strike wings that virtually eliminated all German surface shipping in European waters. The tactic adopted by these wings was based on the use of two waves of aircraft: the aircraft of the first wave sought to destroy the German anti-aircraft defences with rocket fire so that the machines of the second wave could have an uninterrupted run to their torpedo release points; all the aircraft then combined to complete the task with rocket and cannon fire.

The Beaufighter TF.Mk X remained in British service after World War II as the Beaufighter TF.Mk 10, the last aircraft serving in the Far East until retirement in February 1950. A few Beaufighter TF.Mk X aircraft were supplied to Turkey during 1944, and a further batch of 20 was supplied in 1946. The only other countries to fly the Beaufighter TF.Mk X in the post-war period were the Dominican Republic (10 aircraft delivered in 1948 after revision to Beaufighter Mk VI standard with Hercules VI radial engines but no torpedo capability), Israel (four aircraft received clandestinely in 1947), and Portugal (17 aircraft received in 1946).

Beaufighter TT.Mk 10: Between 1948 and 1950, Bristol converted 36 Beaufighter TF.Mk 10 attack fighters to TT.Mk 10 target-towing standard for the RAF. The conversion involved the removal of all armament and radar, and the addition of a target system based on a slipstream-driven windmill projecting from the starboard side of the fuselage and controlled by the observer. The last of these aircraft was retired in May 1960.

Beaufighter Mk XIC: The last variant evolved in the UK, this was a version of the Beaufighter TF.Mk X without torpedo shackles, and production at Weston-super-Mare amounted to 163 aircraft.

Two variants proposed for British production but not actually produced were the Beaufighter Mk VII and Beaufighter Mk XII: the former was planned with turbocharged Hercules VIII radial engines each driving a four-blade propeller; the latter would have been equipped with two Hercules 27 radial engines with Bendix carburettors, and a wing stressed to carry two 1,000lb (454kg) bombs under its outer panels. In fact, the only feature to be used was the revised outer wing arrangement of the Beaufighter Mk XII, which was applied to late-production examples of the Beaufighter TF.Mk X.

DAP Beaufighter: The RAAF evinced an interest in the Beaufighter from an early stage, for its reliable twin-engined powerplant, heavy firepower and good overall performance were attractive features to a force that was growing in size and facing the possibility of Japanese attack from the north (and in a region that was both inhospitable and lacking a network of airfields within short range of each other).

A measure of the Beaufighter's capabilities against the Japanese was provided after September 1942, when the RAAF's No. 27 Squadron re-formed on the Beaufighter Mks IF and VIF. Later reinforced by No. 176 Squadron, No. 27 Squadron was able to take the war to the Japanese in a fashion unmatched by any other British warplane in the Far Eastern theatre. In due course these early fighters were supplemented by Beaufighter Mk X attack fighters, which continued the work of devastating Japanese communications at long range and with the pinpoint accuracy made possible by very-low-level attacks.

Australia's first Beaufighters were imported British aircraft, starting with 72 Beaufighter Mk IC warplanes delivered from April 1942, and followed by 64, 62 and 20 examples of the Beaufighter Mk VIC, Mk X and Mk XIC respectively for delivery in the period up to August 1945. The Australian government was rightly concerned that the RAAF would not be able to obtain sufficient Beaufighters from British sources, however, and in January 1943 decided to undertake production of the Beaufighter in succession to the Beaufort currently being built at the DAP Fishermen's Bend facility. Complete drawings of the Beaufighter were transmitted to Australia, which intended to make the whole airframe and rely on Britain only for supplies of the Hercules radial engine.

The DAP initially planned to produce the Beaufighter Mk VII (different from the British Mk VII) derivative of the Beaufighter Mk VIC with a powerplant of two Hercules 26 (Bendix-carburetted Hercules VI) radial engines, but became concerned that engine supplies could be interrupted. Consequently, one of the RAAF's Beaufighter Mk ICs was experimentally revised with a powerplant of two Wright GR-2600-A5B Cyclone 14 radial piston engines as the aerodynamic prototype of a proposed Beaufighter Mk VIII. The conversion with the larger American engine required the nacelles to be increased in diameter and lengthened to points behind the wing trailing edges. The Beaufighter Mk IX would have been a development of the Mk VIII, with Youngman dive brakes and provision for underwing rocket armament.

The Beaufighter Mks VII, VIII and IX did not materialise, however, for deliveries of the Hercules radial engine were not interrupted, and the DAP therefore opted for a version of the Beaufighter TF.Mk X with a powerplant of two Hercules XVIII radial engines: this engine was a derivative of the Hercules XVII with the two-speed blowers restored to full operation so that the engine delivered its best power outputs at higher altitudes. Other changes adopted for what now became the Beaufighter Mk 21 were removal of the torpedo shackles, radar and dorsal fin fillet; replacement of the six 0.303in (7.7mm) machine-guns in the wings by four 0.5in (12.7mm) Browning machine-guns with their barrels projecting slightly forward of the wing leading edges; and addition of a bulge in the nose immediately forward of the windscreen for a Sperry autopilot that was in fact seldom fitted.

The first Beaufighter Mk 21 flew in May 1944, and deliveries began just a few days later to an eventual total of five RAAF squadrons. Production of the Beaufighter Mk 21 totalled 364 machines by the end of 1945, and another 86 were cancelled at this time. The Beaufighter Mk 21 remained in Australian service until December 1957, latterly in the target-towing role.

Douglas SBD Dauntless

Manufacturer: Douglas Aircraft Company

Country of origin: USA

Specification: SBD-5 Dauntless

Type: Carrierborne and land-based scout and dive-bomber

Accommodation: Pilot and observer/gunner in tandem in an enclosed cockpit

Entered service: Late 1940

Left service: 1959

Armament (fixed): Two 0.5in (12.7mm) Browning M2 fixed forward-firing machine-guns in the upper side of the nose with a synchronisation system to fire through the propeller disc, and two 0.3in (7.62mm) Browning trainable rearward-firing machine-guns in the rear cockpit

Armament (disposable): Up to 2,250lb (1,021kg) of disposable stores carried on three hardpoints (one under the fuselage rated at 1,600lb/726kg and two under the wings with each unit rated at 325lb/147kg), and generally comprising one 1,600 or 1,000lb (726 or 454kg) bomb and two 325lb (147kg) bombs

Operational equipment: Standard communication and navigation equipment, plus optical bomb sights and gunsights

Powerplant: One Wright R-1820-60 Cyclone radial piston engine rated at 1,200hp (895kW) for take-off

Fuel capacity: Internal fuel 258.1 Imp gal (1,173.5 litres); external fuel up to 96.6 Imp gal (439.1 litres) in two drop tanks

Dimensions: Span 41ft 6.375in (12.66m); aspect ratio 5.31; area 325.00sq ft (30.19sq m); length 33ft 1.25in (10.09m); height 13ft 7in (4.14m)

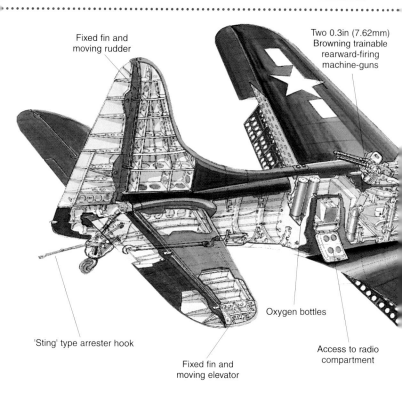

Fixed fin and moving rudder

Two 0.3in (7.62mm) Browning trainable rearward-firing machine-guns

'Sting' type arrester hook

Fixed fin and moving elevator

Oxygen bottles

Access to radio compartment

The Douglas SBD Dauntless was the American equivalent of the Aichi D3A, and as such was the most important carrierborne dive-bomber of the US Navy in the early part of the USA's involvement in World War II.

Weights: Empty 6,404lb (2,905kg) equipped; normal take-off 9,359lb (4,245kg); maximum take-off 10,700lb (4,853kg)

Performance: Maximum level speed 'clean' 221kt (255mph; 410km/h) at 14,000ft (4,267m); cruising speed 161kt (185mph; 298km/h) at optimum altitude; maximum range 1,359nm (1,565 miles; 2,519km) with drop tanks; typical range 968nm (1,115 miles; 1,794km) with typical warload; maximum rate of climb at sea level 1,700ft (518m) per minute; service ceiling 25,530ft (7,780m)

Variants
SBD-1 Dauntless: The Dauntless was one of the decisive warplanes of World War II, despite the fact that it possessed only indifferent performance (especially in climb rate and manoeuvrability) and was phased out of first-line service

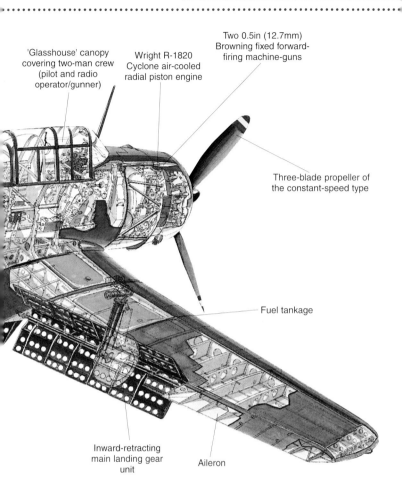

'Glasshouse' canopy covering two-man crew (pilot and radio operator/gunner)

Wright R-1820 Cyclone air-cooled radial piston engine

Two 0.5in (12.7mm) Browning fixed forward-firing machine-guns

Three-blade propeller of the constant-speed type

Fuel tankage

Inward-retracting main landing gear unit

Aileron

well before the end of the war. If it is remembered for nothing else, however, the Dauntless has a secure place in history as one of the victors in the Battle of Midway (June 1942), which was the world's first strategic sea battle between carrierborne forces and resulted in a decisive victory for the US Navy, as its aircraft sank four Japanese aircraft carriers for the loss of only one of their own. The US triumph at Midway switched the strategic initiative from the Imperial Japanese Navy to the US Navy, and for this the small Dauntless was largely responsible. The type was operated from land bases as well as from aircraft carriers, and although the type was to have been replaced from late

The Douglas SBD Dauntless carried its bomb under the fuselage, a crutch (just visible) ensuring that the weapon was swung clear of the turning propeller before it was released just before or during the dive-bomber's exit from a dive.

1944 by the larger Curtiss SB2C Helldiver, the latter's development problems allowed the Dauntless to be retained as a first-line asset until the end of World War II.

The origins of the Dauntless can be found in the Northrop BT-1, which was a first-generation carrierborne scout and dive-bomber characterised by the use of main landing gear units that semi-retracted rearward into large underwing fairings. Northrop was aware that such a scheme offered a considerable reduction in drag by comparison with fixed landing gear units, but also appreciated that landing gear units that retracted fully rather than partially would offer still greater advantages. Northrop recommended to the US Navy the evolution of such landing gear for the BT, and in November 1936 the service instructed the manufacturer to complete one of the current order for 54 BT-1s as the XBT-2 prototype with main landing gear units that fully retracted inward into wells created in the lower surfaces of the wings.

Deck crew prepare Douglas SBD Dauntless carrierborne dive-bombers for take-off from the aircraft carrier USS Yorktown in April 1942, just before the decisive Battle of Midway (June 1942) when the power of the Imperial Japanese navy's carrier force was effectively broken.

Designed under the supervision of 'Ed' Heinemann, the XBT-2 made its first flight in April 1938 with the same powerplant as the standard BT-1, namely a Pratt & Whitney R-1535-94 Twin Wasp Junior radial piston engine rated at 825hp (615kW) and driving a two-blade propeller. The XBT-2 revealed better performance than the BT-1 during early trials, but was damaged in the course of a wheels-up landing. Northrop was currently being absorbed into the Douglas Aircraft Company as its El Segundo Division, and in June 1938 it received instructions from the US Navy that the XBT-2 was not only to be repaired but also fitted with an uprated powerplant in the form of one Wright R-1820-G133 Cyclone radial piston engine rated at 1,000hp (746kW) and driving a three-blade propeller.

When delivered for official trials, the XBT-2 revealed a maximum level speed of 230.5kt (265.5mph; 427km/h), which was 6.5kt (7.5mph; 12km/h) faster than the guaranteed speed and 28.25kt (32.5mph; 52km/h) faster than the standard BT-1. At the end of its official tests, the XBT-2 was delivered to a National Advisory Committee for Aeronautics (NACA) experimental establishment for full-scale wind tunnel tests designed to yield the data required for further enhancement of maximum speed and improvement of the type's stalling characteristics. The NACA team recommended a number of performance-enhancing wing and fuselage modifications, including the improvement of the

external finish and the fairing out of the necked fuselage section created by the incorporation of the larger-diameter R-1820 engine, and these were added in the production model that was to emerge from the XBT-2.

Considerable effort was also made to improve the XBT-2's stability and control, and this involved the construction and evaluation of 21 different rudder/elevator combinations and at least 12 different aileron layouts before the final control-surface configuration was adopted, together with fixed leading-edge slots in the wings ahead of the ailerons, and a dorsal fin between the rear fuselage and fixed fin for improved directional stability. Despite the fact that it had recommended them for the BT-1 as a means of curing a tail unit buffeting problem, the NACA team also recommended the elimination of the type's perforated flaps/dive brakes in order to reduce drag and improve speed despite the revived threat of tail unit buffet, but this suggestion was not adopted.

These improvements were tested on the XBT-2, which thus became increasingly representative of the production type that was ordered in April 1939 to the extent of 36 aircraft. As Northrop was now an intrinsic part of Douglas, which had converted its 51 per cent shareholding into a 100 per cent shareholding as a result of Northrop's continued labour problems, it was decided that the new type should be redesignated to reflect this fact, and the production version of the Northrop XBT-2 thus became the Douglas SBD-1.

This was modelled closely on the XBT-2 with such additional improvements as the R-1820-32 radial engine rated at 1,000hp (746kW), the addition of two 12.5 Imp gal (56.8 litre) tanks in the centre section, and the doubling of the fixed forward-firing armament by the addition of a second 0.5in (12.7mm) Browning machine-gun on the upper decking of the forward fuselage. The first of these new aircraft was completed in April 1940 and made its initial flight at the beginning of May before being delivered to the US Navy in September of the same year; the last of 57 SBD-1s was completed in December 1940. The SBD-1 carried a disposable load of up to 1,000lb (454kg) on its underfuselage hardpoint, which was fitted with a crutch to swing the bomb clear of the propeller disc before the weapon was released, and the two underwing hardpoints each carried a rack for one 100lb (45kg) bomb. In other respects, the variant differed from the SBD-5 in details such as its length of 32ft 2in (9.80m); empty weight of 5,903lb (2,678kg); maximum take-off weight of 9,790lb (4,441kg);

Seen in October 1943, these Douglas SBD Dauntless dive-bombers of the VS-6 squadron are passing over their parent ship, the aircraft carrier USS Enterprise.

maximum level speed of 220kt (253mph; 407km/h) at optimum altitude; cruising speed of 123kt (142mph; 228km/h) at optimum altitude; maximum range of 1,012nm (1,165 miles; 1,875km) on a scouting mission; typical range of 747nm (860 miles; 1,384km) on a bombing mission; initial climb rate of 1,730ft (527m) per minute, and service ceiling of 29,600ft (9,020m).

The SBD-1 entered service initially with VMB-2, a land-based squadron of the US Marine Corps which received its first aircraft in late 1940. Within 12 months, another four squadrons (three of the US Navy and another one of the US Marine Corps) had formed on the Dauntless, and these five units were the US Navy's most potent dive-bomber at the time of Pearl Harbor. Eight SBD-1s were modified in service to a photo-reconnaissance standard with the revised designation SBD-1P Dauntless.

SBD-2 Dauntless: The 57 examples of the SBD-1 were followed by 87 examples of the SBD-2 delivered between December 1940 and May 1941 for the exclusive use of US Navy squadrons. The primary change in this dedicated over-water model was an increase in the fuel capacity to 258.1 Imp gal (1,173.5 litres) by the replacement of the two 12.5

Imp gal (56.8 litre) tanks in the centre section by two 54.1 Imp gal (246.1 litre) tanks in the outer wing panels. (Once the value of self-sealing fuel tanks had been confirmed by operational use, some of the SBD-2s were fitted with such tanks even though this meant a reduction in capacity to 216.5 Imp gal/984.2 litres). Performance was adversely affected by the increased fuel weight, and one of the 0.5in (12.7mm) fixed forward-firing machine-guns was sacrificed in an effort to mitigate this reduction in capability. In other respects, the SBD-2 differed from the SBD-5 in details such as its length of 32ft 2in (9.80m); empty weight of 5,652lb (2,564kg); normal take-off weight of 8,643lb (3,920kg); maximum take-off weight of 10,360lb (4,699kg); maximum level speed of 222kt (256mph; 412km/h) at 16,000ft (4,877m); cruising speed of 128kt (147mph; 237km/h) at optimum altitude; maximum range of 1,190nm (1,370 miles; 2,205km) on a scouting mission; typical range of 1,064nm (1,225 miles; 1,971km) on a bombing mission; initial climb rate of 1,080ft (329m) per minute, and service ceiling of 27,260ft (8,310m).

At least 15 SBD-2s were modified to photo-reconnaissance standard with the revised designation SBD-2P Dauntless.

SBD-3 Dauntless: The SBD-1 and SBD-2 versions of the Dauntless must be regarded with hindsight as service development machines rather than fully combat-capable warplanes, for they lacked many of the features that had already been seen as vital in European operations during the first year of World War II. This fact was signalled by the US Navy in September 1940 when it ordered the SBD-3 not only in larger numbers (585 aircraft in all) but also with improved features such as fully self-sealing fuel tankage, armour protection for the crew and vital equipment, and a return to the SBD-1's heavier fixed forward-firing armament; improved defensive capability was later retrofitted with the adoption of twin 0.3in (7.62mm) belt-fed Browning machine-guns in place of the original single magazine-fed weapon. Other changes were the removal of flotation equipment, and the replacement of Dural by Alclad skinning.

The first SBD-3 was delivered in March 1942, and in other respects this variant differed from the SBD-5 in details such as its powerplant of one R-1820-52 Cyclone radial engine rated at 1,000hp (746kW); length of 32ft 8in (9.96m); empty weight of 6,345lb (2,878kg); maximum take-off weight of 10,400lb (4,717kg); maximum level speed of 217kt (250mph; 402km/h) at optimum altitude; cruising speed of 132kt (152mph; 245km/h) at optimum altitude; maximum range of 1,372nm (1,580 miles; 2,543km) on a scouting mission; typical range of 1,168nm (1,345 miles; 2,165km) on a bombing mission; initial climb rate of 1,190ft (363m) per minute, and service ceiling of 27,100ft (8,260m).

Some 47 of the aircraft were modified in service as photo-reconnaissance machines with the revised designation SBD-3P Dauntless.

The first of a flight of three Douglas SBD Dauntless dive-bombers tips its nose down at the beginning of a dive attack during operations in the Pacific theatre during December 1943, when the Dauntless was approaching total obsolescence as a first-line warplane.

The Douglas SBD Dauntless dive-bomber was most important to the US Navy in the middle of 1942, when the type played a major part in destroying the Japanese navy's aircraft-carrier capability, and then started taking the war to Japan's remaining warships and island bases after the Americans had seized the strategic initiative.

SBD-4 Dauntless: The considerable improvement in the SBD-3's operational capabilities derived in part from the variant's upgraded systems, and this placed a great strain on the type's 12-volt electrical system, which had been inherited from the simpler BT-1. The decision was therefore taken to revise the basic aeroplane with a 24-volt electrical system in the SBD-4 version, which retained the R-1820-52 engine but driving a new Hamilton Standard Hydromatic constant-speed propeller.

The first SBD-4 was delivered in October 1942, and production of this variant totalled 780 aircraft to a standard that in other respects differed from that of the SBD-5 in details such as its length of 32ft 8in (9.96m); empty weight of 6,360lb (2,885kg); maximum take-off weight of 10,480lb (4,754kg); maximum level speed of 213kt (245mph; 394km/h) at optimum altitude; cruising speed of 130kt (150mph; 241km/h) at optimum altitude; maximum range of 1,259nm (1,450 miles; 2,333km) on a scouting mission; typical range of 1,129nm (1,300 miles; 2,092km) on a bombing mission; initial climb rate of 1,150ft (351m) per minute, and service ceiling of 26,700ft (8,138m).

Some 16 of the aircraft were modified in service as photo-reconnaissance machines with the revised designation SBD-4P Dauntless.

SBD-5 Dauntless: This was the major production variant of the Dauntless family, and resulted from the US Navy's somewhat belated acceptance of the fact that the SBD-3 and SBD-4 were underpowered and were failing to deliver

adequate performance in such vital areas as climb rate and service ceiling. Consequently, the main change effected in the SBD-5 was the adoption of the R-1820-60 Cyclone radial engine, rated at 1,200hp (895kW) for a 20 per cent boost in available power, in a revised nacelle that lacked the upper-lip inlet that was characteristic of the earlier variants. The new engine improved speed slightly and climb rate more markedly, and also allowed the carriage of a heavier disposable weapons load in the form of one 1,600lb (726kg) armour-piercing bomb on the underfuselage crutch and two 325lb (147kg) bombs under the wings; the twin-gun defensive scheme that was a retrofit on the SBD-4 became a production feature of the SBD-5.

The first SBD-5 was delivered in February 1943, and production totalled 2,964 aircraft.

SBD-5A Dauntless: The US Navy ordered these 60 aircraft for the USAAF, and to a land-based standard of the SBD-5. In fact, the aircraft were delivered from February 1943 to units of the US Marine Corps intended for service on land bases in the Pacific theatre, and differed from the SBD-5 in details such as their USAAF instrumentation and radio equipment, their use of a pneumatic rather than solid tailwheel tyre, and their lack of an arrester hook. This last detail was a feature of all Dauntless derivatives intended for USAAF aircraft.

SBD-6 Dauntless: The last of several SBD-5 contracts had called for the production of 3,000 aircraft, but before the delivery of the first aeroplane, the US Navy modified the contract to cover 1,549 such aircraft with the balance delivered as one XSBD-6 prototype and 1,450 SBD-6 production aircraft. The prototype was needed because the new variant incorporated a number of significant changes from the SBD-5 standard. These included the

Deck crew on the aircraft carrier USS Saratoga ready a Douglas SBD Dauntless dive-bomber for a raid on the headquarters area at Rabaul, the key bastion in Japan's defence of its south-west perimeter, during December 1943.

R-1820-66 radial engine that was rated at 1,350hp (1,007kW) for take-off and 1,200hp (895kW) at 5,500ft (1,676m), and the replacement of the metal fuel tanks with self-sealing liners by self-sealing tanks of non-metal construction with a capacity of 236.5 Imp gal (1,075.1 litres).

The US Navy accepted the XSBD-6 prototype in February 1944, the month in which the order for 1,450 SBD-6 aircraft was trimmed to just 450 machines in final appreciation that the Dauntless had reached the end of its useful development life and was now obsolescent. The 450 aircraft were delivered between March and July 1944, when production of the Dauntless family ended, many of them carrying ASV (air-to-surface vessel) radar with underwing antennae. Such equipment had already been retrofitted to a number of SBD-5s in tacit recognition that the Dauntless was now more useful for the roles of patrol and interdiction of Japan's maritime lines of communication.

In other respects, the SBD-6 differed from the SBD-5 in details such as its empty weight of 6,554lb (2,973kg); maximum take-off weight of 10,882lb (4,936kg); maximum level speed of 228kt (263mph; 423km/h) at optimum altitude; cruising speed of 124kt (143mph; 230km/h) at optimum altitude; maximum range of 1,476nm (1,700 miles; 2,736km) on a scouting mission; typical range of 1,068nm (1,230 miles; 1,979km) on a bombing mission; initial climb rate of 1,710ft (521
m) per minute, and service ceiling of 28,600ft (8,717m).

The A-24 series was the land-based variant of the SBD evolved to meet a requirement of the USAAF, and exported variants of this series were last of the Dauntless models to remain in service. Operator totals for the Dauntless series were France (72+), New Zealand (65), Mexico (about 10), the UK (9) and the USA (5,936).

Fairey Swordfish

Manufacturer: Fairey Aviation Co. Ltd.

Country of origin: UK

Specification: Swordfish Mk I

Type: Carrierborne and land-based torpedo bomber and reconnaissance aeroplane

Accommodation: Pilot, navigator/observer and radio operator/gunner in tandem in two open cockpits

Entered service: July 1936

Left service: May 1945

Armament (fixed): One 0.303in (7.7mm) Vickers fixed forward-firing machine-gun on the starboard side of the forward upper fuselage with synchronisation equipment to fire through the propeller disc, and one 0.303in (7.7mm) Lewis trainable rearward-firing machine-gun with 582 rounds in the rear cockpit

Armament (disposable): Up to 1,600lb (726kg) of disposable stores carried on nine hardpoints (one under

Wholly obsolete by every technical criterion, the Fairey Swordfish was nonetheless one of the most effective maritime attack aircraft of World War II, and was much loved by crews who operated the 'Stringbag' right to the end of the war against Germany.

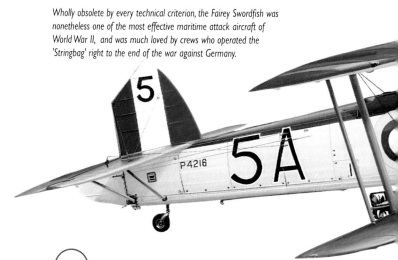

the fuselage rated at 1,600lb/726kg and eight under the wings with each unit of the inboard pair rated at 500lb/227kg, each unit of the two intermediate pairs at 250lb/113kg, and each unit of the outboard pair at 80lb/36kg), and generally comprising one 1,610lb (730kg) torpedo of 18in (457mm) diameter or one 1,500lb (680kg) mine carried under the fuselage, or up to 1,500lb (680kg) of bombs made up of varying numbers of 500, 250 and 20lb (227, 113 and 9.1kg) weapons carried under the fuselage and wings

Operational equipment: Standard communication and navigation equipment, plus optical gunsights and provision for a reconnaissance camera

Powerplant: One Bristol Pegasus IIIM.3 radial piston engine rated at 775hp (578kW) for take-off and 690hp (514kW) at 3,500ft (1,067m)

Fuel capacity: Internal fuel 167.5 Imp gal (761.5 litres) plus provision for up to 69 Imp gal (313.7 litres) of auxiliary fuel in one tank installed in the observer's position or carried on the torpedo crutch; external fuel none

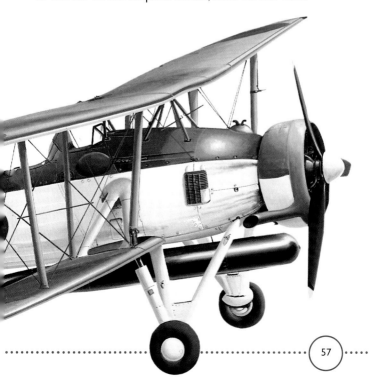

Dimensions: Span 45ft 6in (13.87m) and width folded 17ft 3in (5.26m); area 607.00sq ft (56.39sq m); length 36ft 1in (11.00m) with the tail down or 36ft 4in (11.07m) with the tail up; height 12ft 10.5in (3.92m) with the tail down or 13ft 5.75in (4.11m) with the tail up

Weights: Empty 5,200lb (2,359kg) equipped; normal take-off 8,100lb (3,674kg); maximum take-off 9,250lb (4,196kg)

Performance: Maximum level speed 'clean' 121kt (139mph; 224km/h) at 4,750ft (1,448m) declining to 115kt (132mph; 212km/h) at sea level; cruising speed, maximum 111kt (128mph; 206km/h) at 5,000ft (1524m) and economical 90kt (104mph; 167km/h) at 5,000ft (1,524m); maximum range 894.5nm (1,030 miles; 1,658km) with auxiliary fuel; typical range 474nm (546 miles; 878km) with a 1,500lb (680kg) bomb load; climb to 5,000ft (1,524m) in 10min 30sec; service ceiling 12,400ft (3,780m)

Variants
Swordfish Mk I: The Swordfish has an enduring reputation as one of the finest warplanes of World War II, mainly because it was an anachronism. Not only was it a biplane at a time when the monoplane reigned supreme, but also a biplane of such low performance that it was difficult both for monoplane fighters to fly slow enough to hold fhe type in their sights for more than a fleeting moment and for anti-aircraft guns to track the type with sights calibrated for use against faster warplanes. But the Swordfish was also rugged, reliable, versatile in terms of weapons and equipment, and possessed such superb handling characteristics that it could be flown in most weather conditions and from all sizes of aircraft carrier. The finest accolades for the Swordfish must be the two facts that it outlived by some two years of first-line service its planned successor, the Fairey Albacore, and sank a greater tonnage of Axis shipping than any other Allied warplane.

The origins of this classic aeroplane can be traced to the Air Ministry's June 1930 release of the S.9/30 requirement for a carrierborne aircraft able to operate in two roles – as a three-seat spotter and reconnaissance machine and as a two-seat torpedo bomber. Fairey's design team, headed by Marcel Lobelle with H.E. Chaplin as its chief engineer and aerodynamicist, was already at work on a conceptually similar private-venture design, later given the designation

The Fairey Swordfish carrierborne torpedo bomber is seen in its typical milieu: low and slow, with the torpedo just released from the shackles below the fuselage and falling almost horizontally into the water.

TSR I (Torpedo Spotter Reconnaissance type I), for which the Greek navy was thought likely to be the first purchaser. The private-venture prototype was a large two-bay biplane with fixed tailwheel landing gear including main units of the divided type, and made its maiden flight in March 1933 with a powerplant of one Armstrong Siddeley Panther VI radial piston engine rated at 625hp (466kW) and driving a two-blade Fairey-Reed metal propeller of the fixed-pitch type.

After the completion of initial trials, this engine was replaced by a Bristol Pegasus IIM radial piston engine rated at 635hp (473.5kW) and installed in a narrow-chord Townend ring cowling. The revision of the powerplant coincided with the introduction of the TSR I designation, and trials resumed in July 1933. Initial results were promising, but in September the TSR I was lost after entering a flat spin from which recovery proved impossible.

As final assembly of the private-venture prototype was proceeding in January 1933, Fairey provided full details of this type to the Air Ministry as a possibility for further development as a torpedo bomber and spotter/reconnaissance type for the Fleet Air Arm. Meanwhile, the company was undertaking the detail design and construction of its S.9/30 prototype. (In October 1930 the

Appearing somewhat the worse for the wear and tear of operational conditions, these Fairey Swordfish torpedo bombers nonetheless look serviceable and ready for battle with an armament of one torpedo and provision under their lower wings for rocket projectiles.

company had submitted three proposals to the Air Ministry, and one of these had been selected for prototype evaluation against the Gloster FS.36).

The S.9/30 design was based on a fabric-covered structure of stainless steel, and on a fuselage built in four sections for ease of maintenance and repair. This oval-section structure carried the fixed tailwheel landing gear with its main units of the divided type, the strut/wire-braced tail unit, and the unequal-span biplane wing cellule. This last feature was staggered, designed to fold rearward from narrow-chord centre sections without the need for jury struts, and carried trailing-edge Frise ailerons and leading-edge Handley Page slots on its upper surfaces. Other features of the design were a fixed armament of two 0.303in (7.7mm) machine-guns in the form of a Vickers fixed forward-firing weapon in the forward fuselage and a Lewis trainable rearward-firing weapon in the rear cockpit, a disposable armament of one torpedo carried under the fuselage or bombs carried under the lower wings, and a powerplant of one Rolls-Royce Kestrel IIMS Vee piston engine rated at 525hp (391kW), driving a two-blade Fairey-Reed metal propeller of the fixed-pitch type, and steam-cooled by surface radiators below the upper-wing centre section.

The S.9/30 was first flown in 1934 as a landplane, but then revised for 1935 trials as a floatplane with a large central float and two smaller underwing stabilising floats. The S.9/30 handled well on the water but less well in the air, and by this time the revised S.15/33 specification had been issued and Fairey had decided to offer an improved version of the TSR I as the TSR II with a longer rear fuselage, spin-recovery strakes on the fuselage sides ahead of the tailplane, the outer wing panels swept back at 4 degrees to preserve the relationship of the centre of lift and the centre of gravity despite the lengthening of the rear fuselage, and the vertical tail surface increased in chord.

The new type retained basically the same structure as the TSR I, and was therefore based on a fuselage whose oval section was created by fairing out a rectangular core structure of steel, the whole being covered in quickly detachable light-alloy panels forward and fabric aft. From front to rear, this structure carried the powerplant, oil and fuel tanks, and the tandem one-seat pilot's and two-seat navigator's and gunner's cockpits. The rear fuselage carried the tail unit, which was of fabric-covered steel and Dural construction and comprised the combination of a strut-braced horizontal surface and wire-braced vertical surface, while the central fuselage carried the unequal-span biplane wing cellule. This was based on upper- and lower-wing centre sections of narrow chord separated at their outer ends by interplane struts: the lower-wing centre section extended from the lower longerons and was braced to the upper longeron on each side by an inverted-Vee strut, and the upper-wing centre section curved upward in its thinner central portion and was carried above the fuselage on an arrangement of cabane struts. These centre sections carried the outer wing panels, which were designed to fold to the rear on rear-spar hinges: these panels, like the centre sections, were of fabric-covered steel and Dural con-struction, carried ailerons that could be drooped collectively as flaps on the outboard ends of all four surfaces' trailing edges, sported slots on the outboard ends of the upper panels' leading edges, were separated by outward sloping interplane struts, and were braced by the standard arrangement of flying and landing wires. The airframe was completed by the fixed tailwheel landing gear with its associated arrester hook under the rear fuselage, and included divided main units each based on a Vee strut whose open end was hinged to the lower longeron on its own side and whose outboard end was braced vertically to the lower-wing centre section by a leg incorporating an oleo-pneumatic shock absorber: the main landing gear units were able to carry either wheels or a side-by-side arrangement of single-step floats.

The TSR II prototype made its maiden flight in April 1934 with a powerplant of one Bristol Pegasus IIIM.3 radial piston engine rated at 690hp (514kW), installed inside a narrow-chord Townend ring cowling and driving a two-blade propeller of the fixed-pitch type: both Watts wooden and Fairey-Reed metal propellers were tested during the prototype's trials, but a three-blade Fairey-Reed metal propeller was selected for the production version of this important warplane. The prototype encountered a fair measure of small-scale criticism during its official trials, but this was concerned mostly with behaviour near the stall, which was cured by comparatively straightforward modification of the control surfaces and their ranges of movement.

At the successful end of its official trials the TSR II was given the official name 'Swordfish', and in April and May 1935 it was ordered to an initial extent of three pre-production and 86 Swordfish Mk I production aircraft. The three pre-production aircraft were completed between December 1935 and mid-1936 for use in development trials, and the Swordfish Mk I entered service in July 1936 with 825 Squadron. By this time it was clear that production of the Swordfish would be too great for Fairey (which was also delivering the Battle light bomber and developing the Albacore torpedo bomber), so at the suggestion of the Admiralty, Blackburn Aircraft Ltd., of Brough in Yorkshire was made responsible for the major portion of Swordfish production, which eventually totalled 2,391 aircraft including 692 made by Fairey: Blackburn delivered one aeroplane in 1940, 415 in 1941, 271 in 1942, 592 in 1943 and a final 420 in 1944.

At the outbreak of World War II the FAA had 13 first-line Swordfish squadrons, and another 12 were formed in the course of the war. The Swordfish was also operated by 22 second-line squadrons and 11 catapult flights that were eventually merged into No. 700 Squadron. Even after the start of World War II, it was to be seven months before the Swordfish saw action for the first time, in the course of the Norwegian campaign of April 1940. In this

This is a Fairey Swordfish Mk II, with a strengthened and metal-skinned lower wing for the carriage of rocket projectiles as a boost to the type's punch in the anti-ship role, although the rockets were also effective in the anti-submarine task.

action, Swordfish aircraft of Nos 816 and 818 Squadrons made the first co-ordinated torpedo attack in the history of air warfare: the attack's intended targets were two German cruisers at Trondheim, but in their absence, the aircraft attacked two destroyers, sinking one of them. Only two days later, one Swordfish achieved a remarkable feat during the 1st Battle of Narvik: spotting for the 15in (381mm) guns of the battleship HMS *Warspite*, the aeroplane performed so well that the battleship and her escorting destroyers sank or caused the scuttling of seven German destroyers, and the Swordfish then dive-bombed and sank a German submarine. By this time other squadrons were heavily involved in the British minelaying effort, and also in the bombing of German-held ports together with the coastal shipping plying between them.

After Italy's entry into World War II in June 1940, Swordfish aircraft based on Malta started to play havoc with Italy's Mediterranean shipping: over a period of seven months, a force that never exceeded 27 aircraft sank a monthly average of more than 50,000 tons. Undoubtedly the greatest feat of the Swordfish, however, was the crippling of the Italian fleet in Taranto harbour: for the loss of only two aircraft, 20 aircraft attacked by night and succeeded in sinking the battleship RN *Conte di Cavour*, severely damaging two other battleships including one that had to be beached, severely damaging two cruisers, damaging two destroyers and sinking two auxiliary vessels.

Further credits to the Swordfish in its primary torpedo-bombing role included the crippling of the German battleship KMS *Bismarck* during her Atlantic sortie of May 1941, allowing British surface forces to close and sink her, and the gallant but hopeless attempt by No. 825 Squadron (which lost all six of its aircraft and 13 out of 18 men) to cripple the German battle-cruisers KMS *Scharnhorst* and *Gneisenau*, together with the heavy cruiser KMS *Prinz Eugen*, as they ran up the English Channel from Brest in north-western France to Germany during February 1942. This was the last major torpedo bomber effort made by the Swordfish, which came increasingly into its own as a rocket-armed destroyer of coastal shipping and submarines. Production of the Swordfish Mk I totalled 992 aircraft delivered by Fairey and Blackburn, to the extent of 692 and 300 aircraft respectively.

Swordfish Mk II: Built by Blackburn to the total of 1,080 aircraft, this was a development of the Swordfish Mk I, with a strengthened lower wing and metal-skinned undersurfaces for the carriage of eight air-to-surface rockets. These could be of two types, namely the 60lb (27.2kg) high-explosive or 25lb (11.3kg) armour-piercing models. The former was notably effective against coastal shipping and the latter against submarines and coastal fortifications.

Swordfish Mk III: Built by Blackburn to the total of 320 aircraft, this was a development of the Swordfish Mk II, with improved anti-submarine capability bestowed by the addition of ASV.Mk X air-to-surface search radar with its antenna in a large radome under the fuselage between the main landing gear legs. The Swordfish Mks II and III were identical with the Swordfish Mk I in all significant respects of dimensions and performance, but differed in details such as their empty weight of 4,700lb (2,132kg), normal take-off weight of 6,750lb (3,062kg), and maximum take-off weight of 9,250lb (4,196kg).

The Swordfish Mks II and III performed excellently whilst operating off escort carriers protecting Atlantic and Arctic convoys against German submarine attack, and the last FAA Swordfish unit was No. 836 Squadron that was disbanded in May 1945 just after the surrender of Germany.

Swordfish Mk IV: This designation was applied to a few Swordfish Mk II aircraft converted with enclosed cockpits for use over the cold waters off the eastern coast of Canada.

Grumman G-40 (TBF Avenger)

Manufacturer: Grumman Aircraft Engineering Corporation

Country of origin: USA

Specification: TBF-1C Avenger

Type: Carrierborne torpedo and level bomber

Accommodation: Pilot, navigator/ventral gunner and radio operator/dorsal gunner in tandem in an enclosed cockpit

Entered service: May 1942

Left service: April 1966

Armament (fixed): Two 0.5in (12.7mm) Browning M2 fixed forward-firing machine-guns in the wing leading edges with 600 rounds per gun, one 0.5in (12.7mm) Browning M2 trainable rearward-firing machine-gun in the power-operated dorsal turret with 400 rounds, and one 0.3in (7.62mm) Browning trainable rearward-firing machine-gun in the ventral position with 500 rounds

Armament (disposable): Up to 2,500lb (1,134kg) of disposable stores carried in a lower-fuselage weapons bay rated at 2,000lb (907kg) and on two hardpoints (both under the wings with each unit rated at 250lb/113kg), and generally comprising one 22in (559mm) Mk 13-2 torpedo, or one 1,600 or 1,000lb (726 or 454kg) bomb or four 500lb (227kg) bombs carried in the weapons bay, and up to eight 5in (127mm) HVAR rockets carried under the wings

Operational equipment: Standard communication and navigation equipment, plus a Norden torpedo/bomb sight, optical gunsights, and provision for ASB (air-to-surface type B) radar using Yagi antennae or APS-4 search radar with its antenna in a pod under the starboard wing

Powerplant: One Wright R-2600-8 Cyclone 14 radial piston engine rated at 1,700hp (1,268kW) up to 3,000ft

The Grumman TBF Avenger had good performance and armament, and was especially notable for its protection and great structural strength.

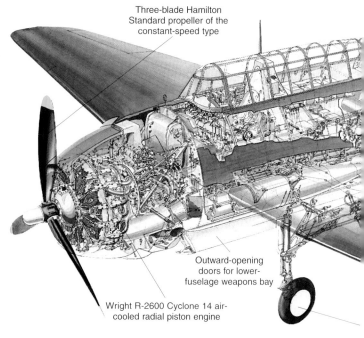

Three-blade Hamilton Standard propeller of the constant-speed type

Outward-opening doors for lower-fuselage weapons bay

Wright R-2600 Cyclone 14 air-cooled radial piston engine

(914m) and 1,450hp (1,081kW) between 7,800 and 12,000ft (2,377 and 3,657m)

Fuel capacity: Internal fuel 279 Imp gal (1,268.1 litres) plus provision for 229 Imp gal (1,041 litres) of auxiliary fuel in a jettisonable weapons-bay tank; external fuel up to 96.6 Imp gal (439.1 litres) in two drop tanks

Dimensions: Span 54ft 2in (16.51m) and width folded 19ft 0in (5.79m); aspect ratio 4.99; area 490.00sq ft (45.52sq m); length 40ft 9in (12.42m); height 13ft 9in (4.19m) with the tail down; wheel track 10ft 10in (3.30m)

Weights: Empty 10,555lb (4,788kg) equipped; normal take-off 16,412lb (7,444kg); maximum take-off 17,364lb (7,876kg)

Performance: Maximum level speed 'clean' 223kt (257mph; 414km/h) at 12,000ft (3,657m) declining to 216kt (249mph; 401km/h) at sea level; cruising speed, economical 133kt (153mph; 246km/h) at optimum altitude;

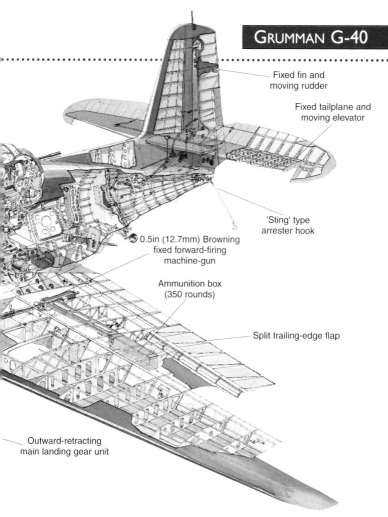

Fixed fin and
moving rudder

Fixed tailplane and
moving elevator

'Sting' type
arrester hook

0.5in (12.7mm) Browning
fixed forward-firing
machine-gun

Ammunition box
(350 rounds)

Split trailing-edge flap

Outward-retracting
main landing gear unit

maximum range 2,332nm (2,685 miles; 4,321km) with
auxiliary fuel and drop tanks; typical range 960nm (1,105
miles; 1,778km) with internal fuel; climb to 10,000ft
(3,048m) in 13min 0sec; service ceiling 21,400ft (6,523m)

Variants

TBF-1 Avenger: The Avenger was a disastrous
disappointment during its combat debut in the Battle of
Midway of June 1942, when it suffered the loss of five out of
six aircraft as a result of the inexperience of its crews, but
then matured as one of the decisive weapons of World War
II in the hands of the US Navy and the Royal Navy. The type
proved itself to be enormously flexible in its offensive
capabilities against warships and their supporting auxiliaries,
submarines and merchant ships, and in defensive terms the

type was aided by its immense strength and its design similarity to Grumman single-seat fighters, which persuaded many fighter pilots to close from angles well defended by the Avenger's two defensive machine-guns. The Avenger remained in fruitful service and development in the period after the war, and was a valuable asset for the naval air arms of many countries allied to the USA.

The origins of the type can be traced back to March 1939, when the US Navy's Bureau of Aeronautics issued a requirement for a VTB (carrierborne torpedo bomber) to succeed the Douglas TBD Devastator, a first-generation monoplane that had been rendered obsolescent after only 18 months of service. The Bureau of Aeronautics demanded that the winner of its 1939 VTB design competition had to demonstrate its ability to undertake torpedo and bomb attacks on surface ships, lay heavy smokescreens, scout on behalf of the surface forces of the US Navy, and engage light surface ships with weapons such as fixed forward-firing guns.

Within this overall mission requirement, the winning VTB contender had to possess a maximum level speed in excess of 261kt (301mph; 484km/h) with a normal fuel load; a range in excess of 868nm (1,000 miles; 1,609km) while carrying one torpedo or three 500lb (227kg) bombs; a service ceiling of at least 30,000ft (9,144m); good flightdeck performance; a low stalling speed; internal accommodation for the primary weapons load; and dimensions not exceeding a span of 60ft 0in (18.29m), length of 39ft 0in (11.89m) and height of 17ft 0in (5.18m) with the wings folded. The requirement exerted great pressure on the aeronautical state of the art, and was perhaps impossible of attainment in its performance parameters given the technology of the day, but by August 1939 the Bureau of Aeronautics had received no fewer than 13 design submissions from Brewster, Douglas, Grumman, Hall, Vought and Vultee.

Grumman offered two variants of its G-40 concept produced under the design leadership of William T. Schwendler, and these differed mainly in the version of the Wright R-2600 Cyclone 14 radial piston engine installed: one was based on a Cyclone 14 with a single-stage two-speed supercharger for good medium-altitude performance, and the other on a Cyclone 14 with a two-stage two-speed supercharger for improved high-altitude performance. By the autumn of 1939, the Bureau of Aeronautics had discarded 10 of the original 13 design submissions so that it could concentrate on the G-40 version using the Cyclone 14 with

Unwary Japanese pilots were sometimes misled by the similarity of the TBF Avenger's configuration to that of the smaller Grumman single-seat fighter, and then suffered from the attentions of the dorsal and/or ventral gun when making a stern attack.

a two-stage supercharger, as well as a Brewster design with the R-2600 radial engine and a Vought design with the Pratt & Whitney R-2800 Double Wasp radial piston engine.

The Bureau of Aeronautics completed its deliberations in November 1939 and recommended the procurement of one Vought and two Grumman prototypes, the clear indication being that the G-40 was considered the better of the two final contenders. There followed a delay before the prototype contracts were issued, and it was April 1940 before Grumman received its order for two XTBF-1 prototypes.

The next step toward the creation of the real aeroplane was the mock-up, and this was inspected by the relevant US Navy authorities in July 1940. The mock-up revealed the G-40's strong likeness to the G-36 (F4F) carrierborne fighter, although the G-40 was inevitably larger. The major points of similarity were the general shaping of the deep fuselage, the tail unit and the mid-set cantilever wing, and the use of Grumman's 'sto-wing' system in which the tapered outer wing panels folded back along the outer ends of the parallel-chord centre section to lie alongside the rear fuselage rather than upward in the manner of most other modern naval aircraft. All the control surfaces were fabric-covered units, and comprised horn-balanced elevators and a rudder on the tail unit, and ailerons on the wing trailing edges outboard of the otherwise full-span flaps; fixed slots were let into the leading edge of each outer wing panel ahead of inboard three-fifths of the ailerons. A long 'glasshouse' canopy was installed above the wing, its rear terminating in the electrically powered dorsal turret whose single 0.5in

(12.7mm) machine-gun was to provide the most important element of the new warplane's defensive capability, and the weapons bay with hydraulically operated doors was located under the wing. The line of the weapons bay was extended slightly to the rear to provide accommodation for the ventral gunner whose 0.3in (7.62mm) 'stinger' weapon defended against attack from below and behind, and the armament was completed by a single 0.5in (12.7mm) fixed forward-firing machine-gun on the starboard upper side of the forward fuselage with synchronisation equipment so that it could fire through the propeller disc.

The G-40 differed from the G-36 in one major respect, however, and this was the arrangement of the tailwheel landing gear: in the G-36 the narrow-track main units were attached to the fuselage and retracted upward into this structure, but in the G-40 the main units were attached to the wings and retracted outward; the tailwheel and arrester hook were also fully retractable. So far as the main landing gear arrangement was concerned, this meant much greater track and consequent improvement of the G-40's flightdeck handling. Although the powerplant initially selected for the prototype and first production aircraft was the R-2600 in a version with a two-stage two-speed supercharger, development of this engine was running behind schedule and Grumman was forced to adopt the R-2600-8 with a single-stage two-speed supercharger and a three-blade Curtiss Electric metal propeller of the constant-speed type.

Towards the end of 1940 the US Navy was becoming increasingly concerned about its reliance on a small force of TBD-1 Devastator torpedo bombers: the nature of the air war in Europe during 1939 and 1940 had shown that the type was obsolete, and in December 1940 the service ordered 285 examples of the TBF-1 initial production model as well as one XTBF-2 prototype with the R-2600-10 Cyclone 14 radial engine with a two-stage two-speed supercharger.

One of the keys to the Grumman TBF Avenger's good performance was a relatively clean basic design coupled with a powerful radial piston engine driving a substantial three-blade propeller.

The first XTBF-1 made the type's maiden flight in August 1941, seven months after the TBF had been ordered into production, and soon ran into problems as the engine was located not far enough forward to put the centre of gravity in the right position in relation to the centre of lift, the engine suffered cooling problems, and the tail unit was found to lack sufficient vertical area to ensure adequate directional stability. The first prototype was therefore returned to the plant for changes to the engine installation and to the tail unit, but was then lost as a result of an in-flight fire in November 1941. Fortunately, this did not occasion a lengthy delay to the programme, as the second prototype was completed only three weeks later, with the first TBF-1 production-line machine following at the beginning of January 1942. These aircraft were completed with a large dorsal fin that cured the directional instability problem.

By this time the USA had been drawn into World War II by the Japanese attack on Pearl Harbor in December 1941, and in the early days of 1942 the hard-pressed US Navy wanted Grumman to concentrate on basically defensive weapons such as the F4F and F6F fighters that were in service and under development respectively. Offensive

weapons such as the TBF were a longer-term need, even though the TBD was of virtually no operational use, and the US Navy decided that it would be wise to introduce a second production source into the programme. The logical choice was the Eastern Aircraft Division of the General Motors Corporation, whose facility at Linden in New Jersey had already been selected as a second source for production of the F4F (as the FM). Eastern Aircraft was based on five General Motors facilities in the Middle Atlantic states, and the Trenton plant in New Jersey was chosen to assemble aircraft from Grumman-produced parts.

Eastern Aircraft soon assumed primary responsibility for production of this TBF variant (the TBM), with the wings and cowling produced at Tarrytown in New York State, the rear fuselage at Baltimore, the electrical and hydraulic systems at Bloomfield in New Jersey, and the rest of the airframe at Trenton, where final assembly was concentrated. The combination of Grumman and Eastern Aircraft capabilities proved excellent, and the two concerns produced 9,839 production aircraft: Grumman's production peaked in September 1943, when 163 aircraft were delivered, and ended in December 1943 after the construction of 2,293 TBFs; while Eastern Aircraft's production peaked in March 1945, when 400 aircraft were delivered, and ended in September 1945 after the construction of 7,546 TBMs.

The first 2,074 aircraft were completed to the initial production standard as finalised in the second XTBF-1 prototype: 1,524 of these were delivered by Grumman with the designation TBF-1 Avenger and the other 550 came from Eastern Aircraft with the designation TBM-1 Avenger. The key details of the TBF-1 included a powerplant of one R-2600-8 Cyclone 14 radial engine rated at 1,700hp (1,268kW) and supplied with fuel from an internal capacity of 279 Imp gal (1,268.1 litres); span of 54ft 2in (16.51m) with an area of 490.00sq ft (45.52sq m); folded width of 19ft 0in (5.79m); length of 40ft 0in (12.19m); height of 16ft 5in (5.00m); empty weight of 10,080lb (4,572kg); normal take-off weight of 13,667lb (6,199kg); maximum take-off weight of 15,905lb (7,214kg); maximum level speed of 235kt (271mph; 436km/h) at 12,000ft (3,657m); economical cruising speed of 126kt (145mph; 233km/h) at optimum altitude; maximum range of 1,259nm (1,450 miles; 2,333km) as a scout; typical range of 1,055nm (1,215 miles; 1,955km) as a torpedo bomber; initial climb rate of 1,430ft (436m) per minute, and service ceiling of 22,400ft (6,827m).

The first TBF-1s entered service with part of the VT-8 squadron in May 1942, and after working up on the type at Norfolk Naval Air Station in Virginia, the unit flew across the United States to California and thence to Hawaii, where it was to have joined the rest of VT-8 on the carrier USS *Wasp*. This ship was absent in the central Pacific, however, and the aircraft flew on to Midway Island. From here six aircraft took part in the Battle of Midway, in which they failed to score a single hit but suffered the loss of five aircraft shot down and the sixth so badly damaged that it was unserviceable. Analysis of these events suggested that the problem lay not with the Avenger but with the tactics used by its inexperienced crews, and revised tactics had been introduced when the VT-3, VT-7 and VT-8 squadrons attached to the carriers USS *Enterprise*, *Wasp* and *Saratoga* flew 41 Avengers with considerable success during the landing on Guadalcanal in August 1942. From this time until the end of the war, the Avenger was a key part of the US Navy's offensive capability, and operated with a large number of squadrons for fleet operations from fast carriers and for support of amphibious operations from escort carriers.

For greater utility in the anti-ship role, some of the aircraft were modified by the US Navy with ASB or APS-4 air-to-surface radar, and an improved capability in the close-support and anti-ship roles was also provided by the retrofit of zero-length launchers under the outer wing panels for a maximum of eight 5in (127mm) HVAR rockets. Subvariants of the TBF/TBM-1 included the TBF-1J Avenger and TBM-1J Avenger that were Grumman and Eastern Aircraft machines revised for arctic operations with features such as a higher-capacity cabin heater, and the TBF-1P Avenger and TBM-1P Avenger photo-reconnaissance machines that carried a camera package in their weapons bays.

TBF-1B Avenger: Some 402 aircraft of the TBF-1 total were completed to this standard for delivery to the United Kingdom under the terms of the Lend-Lease Act.

TBF-1C Avenger: Built to the extent of 764 aircraft that were supplemented by 2,332 examples of the TBM-1C Avenger from Eastern Aircraft's production line, this variant introduced a revised forward-firing machine-gun armament of two 0.5in (12.7mm) weapons in the wing leading edges outboard of the disc swept by the propeller, and greater range capability through provision for up to 325.6 Imp gal

The long 'glasshouse' canopy of the Grumman TBF Avenger series provided the crew with the good fields of vision that were vital to successful operational deployment of the type.

(1,480.1 litres) of additional fuel in a jettisonable weapons-bay tank and two 48.3 Imp gal (219.6 litre) underwing drop tanks. Many of the aircraft received the same radar and/or rocket launcher modifications as the TBF/TBM-1 series aircraft, and others received more extensive modifications that resulted in a number of separately identified subvariants.

A small number of aircraft were adapted for the photo-reconnaissance role with a camera installation in the weapons bay, and these aircraft received the revised designations TBF-1CP Avenger and TBM-1CP Avenger. The parallel designations TBF-1D Avenger and TBM-1D Avenger were used for aircraft optimised for the anti-submarine role with ASD (air-to-surface type D, later redesignated as APS-3) radar with its antenna in a pod attached to the leading edge of the starboard wing, and armament bolstered by the addition of zero-length launchers for eight 5in (127mm) rockets; some of the aircraft were also fitted with ASB radar using Yagi antennae extending above the wing leading edges.

A number of late-production aircraft were completed to the parallel TBF-1E Avenger and TBM-1E Avenger standards with ASH (air-to-surface type H, later redesignated as APS-4) radar with its antenna in a pod under the starboard wing. Finally there were the TBF-1L Avenger and TBM-1L Avenger with a retractable searchlight mounted in the weapons bay for use in the nocturnal illumination of surfaced submarines: the type saw little operational use as the powerful searchlight made an excellent aiming point for the submarines' anti-aircraft gunners.

TBM-3 Avenger: The sole XTBF-2 prototype had been ordered at the same time as the TBF-1 initial production model, and first flew in May 1942 with the XR-2600-10 Cyclone 14 radial engine originally specified for the TBF-1. This engine was fitted with a two-stage two-speed supercharger, and only limited trials were undertaken as the US Navy had now decided that the Avenger would not operate above medium altitude.

Even so, it was clear that a more powerful engine was required, for the addition of extra equipment had added some 2,750lb (1,247kg) to the normal take-off weight of the TBF/TBM-1C (compared with that of the TBF/TBM-1), and performance was eroded to a significant degree. This loss of performance was in itself unfortunate, but less acceptable was the resulting increase in the take-off run, which made it difficult for the TBF/TBM-1C to operate from the smaller flightdecks of escort carriers. The US Navy and Grumman originally considered a switch of powerplant to the Pratt & Whitney R-2800 Double Wasp radial engine rated at 2,000hp (1,491kW), but then decided to adopt a more powerful variant of the standard R-2600 radial engine, namely the R-2600-20 Cyclone 14 rated at 1,900hp (1,417kW).

The use of this engine required the design of a new cowling with multiple flaps on its trailing edge and an oil cooler built into its lower lip, so the US Navy ordered six prototypes in the form of two XTBF-3s and four XTBM-3s. The first of these machines flew in June 1943, and after the development and evaluation of the new powerplant installation, the aircraft were used for a number of other important experimental tasks. The production type resulting from the XTBF/XTBM-3 prototypes restored performance to TBF/TBM-1 levels and was built only by Eastern Aircraft, which delivered 4,657 aircraft of the TBM-3 series from April 1944. In the course of so large a production run it was inevitable that a number of changes should be incorporated as the lessons of operational experience filtered back to the USA.

The most important of these changes was the addition of an autopilot: this replaced the Norden bomb sight (operations having revealed that level bombing was useless against manoeuvring ship targets and less accurate than a shallow dive attack against stationary targets) and made long-range missions far more endurable for the pilot. The TBM-3 was also adapted into a number of subvariants, some of them being only modest alterations from the TBM-3 baseline standard. Had World War II continued, the TBM-3 would have been followed in production by the TBM-4 with a strengthened airframe to provide a modest dive-bombing capability. This variant was presaged by three XTBM-4 prototypes, the first of which made its maiden flight in June 1945 and revealed its ability to perform 5-g manoeuvres at a maximum weight of 16,000lb (7,258kg).

The two XTBM-6s were experimental aircraft, used in this instance within the US Navy's programme to improve Avenger performance by reducing weight and wing loading: the turret was removed; the ventral step was smoothed neatly into the lines of the rear fuselage; the crew was reduced to just two men; the canopy was revised to allow the accommodation of the second man at its rear with a defensive armament of two 0.3in (7.62mm) trainable rearward-firing machine-guns; ejector exhaust stubs were fitted to the engine; and the wing was revised with 3ft 0in (0.91m) greater span and without leading-edge slots. Useful gains in performance were secured in the flight test programme that started in June 1945, but the programme was overtaken by the end of the war and no production development was contemplated.

TBM-3D Avenger: This designation was applied to TBM-3 aircraft adapted for the anti-submarine role and therefore fitted with the same type of radar equipment as the TBF/TBM-1D. Other changes effected on some of the conversions were the addition of a searchlight under the port wing, and the removal of the dorsal turret with the result that the canopy had to be extended farther to the rear.

TBM-3E Avenger: The last Avenger variant to be placed in production during World War II, this model was delivered from December 1944. Among its features were a fuselage lengthening of 11.5in (0.292m), the installation of APS-4 radar with its antenna in a pod under the starboard wing, and an overall lightening by some 300lb (136kg) achieved by revision of several airframe features and omission of items such as the wing and tailplane de-icing equipment. Later changes were the deletion of the ventral gun, elimination of the rear armour plate (protection being maintained by the provision of a flak suit and two flak curtains) and upgrade of the forward-firing armament by provision under the wings for two packages each containing two 0.5in (12.7mm) machine-guns.

The TBM-3E's details included a span of 54ft 2in (16.51m) with an area of 490.00sq ft (45.52sq m); folded

The Grumman TBF Avenger, seen here in the form of a TBF-1, was one of the classic naval attack warplanes of World War II, and in later forms survived well into the 1950s as an effective carrierborne type.

width of 19ft 0in (5.79m); length of 40ft 11.5in (12.48m); height of 16ft 5in (5.00m); empty weight of 10,545lb (4,783kg); normal take-off weight of 14,160lb (6,423kg); maximum take-off weight of 17,895lb (8,117kg); maximum level speed of 240kt (276mph; 444km/h) at 16,500ft (5,030m); economical cruising speed of 128kt (147mph; 237km/h) at optimum altitude; maximum range of 1,667nm (1,920 miles; 3,090km) as a scout; typical range of 981nm (1,130 miles; 1,819km) as a torpedo bomber; initial climb rate of 2,060ft (628m) per minute, and service ceiling of 30,100ft (9,175m).

After the end of the war, many of these aircraft were modernised to the TBM-3E2 Avenger standard that was identifiable by the replacement of the original and retractable 'stinger' type of arrester hook by an external hook farther forward along the underside of the fuselage. Following the surrender of Japan, the number of Avenger squadrons serving with the US Navy's carrier forces was rapidly reduced and most of the aircraft were reallocated to the US Naval Air Reserve. In November 1946 the 18 surviving Avenger squadrons of the US Navy were redesignated in the VA (carrierborne attack) category, but were not destined to survive much longer, as one of the US Navy's most pressing re-equipment efforts was dedicated to replacement of the Avenger by the Douglas AD Skyraider multi-role attack warplane. The last Avengers to operate in this redesignated role were pulled out of service in 1949, but the type continued in development and service for other roles.